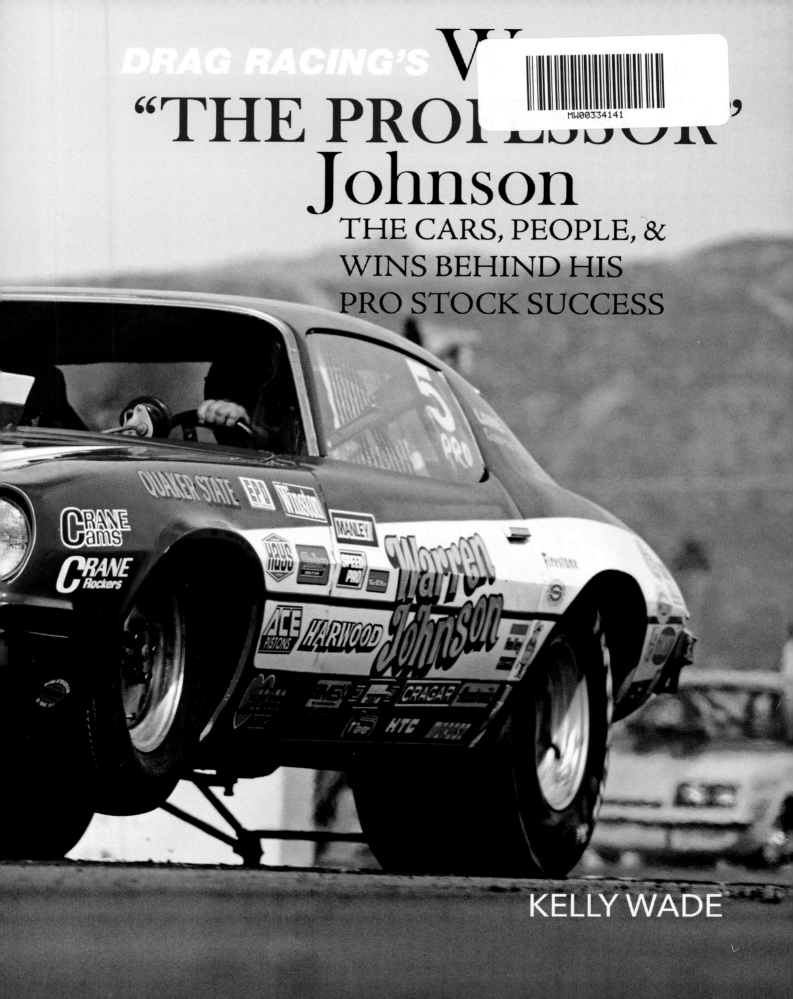

DRAG RACING'S WARREN
"THE PROFESSOR" Johnson
THE CARS, PEOPLE, & WINS BEHIND HIS PRO STOCK SUCCESS

KELLY WADE

CarTech®

CarTech®, Inc.
6118 Main Street
North Branch, MN 55056
Phone: 651-277-1200 or 800-551-4754
Fax: 651-277-1203
www.cartechbooks.com

Edit by Wes Eisenschenk
Layout by Monica Seiberlich

ISBN 978-1-61325-570-4
Item No. CT672

Library of Congress Cataloging-in-Publication Data Available

Written, edited, and designed in the U.S.A.
Printed in China
10 9 8 7 6 5 4 3 2

PUBLISHER'S NOTE: In reporting history, the images required to tell the tale will vary greatly in quality, especially by modern photographic standards. While some images in this volume are not up to those digital standards, we have included them, as we feel they are an important element in telling the story.

DISTRIBUTION BY:

Europe
PGUK
63 Hatton Garden
London EC1N 8LE, England
Phone: 020 7061 1980 • Fax: 020 7242 3725
www.pguk.co.uk

Australia
Renniks Publications Ltd.
3/37-39 Green Street
Banksmeadow, NSW 2109, Australia
Phone: 2 9695 7055 • Fax: 2 9695 7355
www.renniks.com

Canada
Login Canada
300 Saulteaux Crescent
Winnipeg, MB, R3J 3T2 Canada
Phone: 800 665 1148 • Fax: 800 665 0103
www.lb.ca

TABLE OF CONTENTS

Dedication 6

Acknowledgments 6

Introduction 7

Chapter 1: **The Seeds of Speed** 8

Chapter 2: **Family Matters** 18

Chapter 3: **A New Class** 26

Chapter 4: **From Match Racing to a Major Sponsor** 42

Chapter 5: **Crossing the Threshold of Success** 56

Chapter 6: **Magnificent Milestones** 70

Chapter 7: **Domination in the 1990s** 82

Chapter 8: **The Rivalries** 102

Chapter 9: **The Professor's Student** 116

Chapter 10: **Research and Development** 130

Chapter 11: **Comfortable with Controversy** 138

Chapter 12: **Accolades and Adventure** 148

Chapter 13: **Postgrad** 158

Appendix: **Warren Johnson's Lasting Legacy** 174

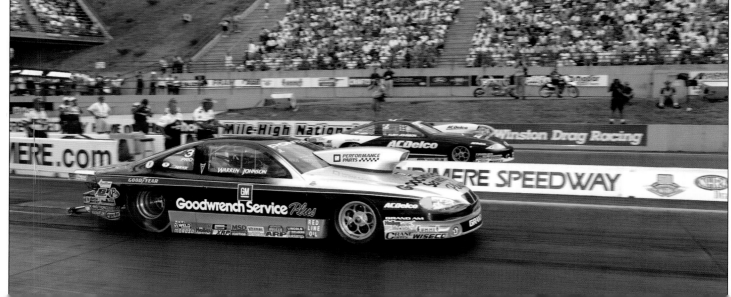

DEDICATION

In memory of Jon Knapp
June 4, 1954–October 22, 2012

ACKNOWLEDGMENTS

My first instinct upon being asked to write this book was to say no. It wasn't that I was too busy or that I thought I didn't know enough about the subject, it was simply that it felt terrifying to even consider writing a book about Warren Johnson, who is a legend in the sport of drag racing and is in a class that I hold in the absolute highest regard.

Our first meeting was in 2007, shortly after I had been hired as an associate editor at the NHRA's *National Dragster*. I'd done a lot of research before my first day on the job, and I was already well aware that Warren Johnson was an icon. At that point in time, he had 96 national event wins and all 6 of his NHRA championships, and he was still diligently plugging along, seemingly unaware of all he'd accomplished.

Jon Knapp, who was managing Warren's public relations at that time with his wife, Joanne Knapp, found it hilarious that I was intimidated. "He's harmless! You'll love him," Jon assured me as he steered me by the shoulders to the back of the team's race trailer. Warren was looking back and forth between notes in front of him and a graph on the computer, and he did not turn his gaze toward us as we approached. I was awash with fear. It felt like I was interrupting a secret meeting.

Jon introduced me, and I searched through my brain for a word or two but found it completely shut down, paralyzed with fear. Warren looked at me and said, nearly growling, "What's the matter? I'm not going to bite you!" I sputtered for a split second before he broke the tension with a genuine laugh, and then his whole demeanor changed. He was friendly and jovial, and from then on, he said something to make me laugh every time I saw him.

The first person to tell me that I should write the Warren Johnson book was Randy Chambers, who worked on Warren's crew and at his shop from 2008 until 2017. I was flattered to hear that someone from inside Warren Johnson Enterprises thought I could take on such a task, but I did not believe I was the right person to do it—mainly because Jon Knapp had worked closely with Warren for many years, held all the stats and insider knowledge, and

was a great writer. This book belonged to Jon, and if he had not passed away in 2012, he would be the one writing this preface after putting together one heck of a tome.

To Warren Johnson, there are no words that can convey my appreciation for your willingness to answer every question I've thrown at you. Your patience throughout this project, particularly when I would call unexpectedly for a lengthy chat or interrupt dinner by pulling out my tape recorder, is what allowed this to work. You are an extraordinary human, and one that I am so fortunate to know.

Arlene Johnson, your name should be on the cover of this book right along with Warren's. I never truly understood all that you did, and now that I do, I hold you in even higher regard. Thank you, from the bottom of my heart, for allowing me to take up so much space in your life and for treating me so kindly. You welcomed me with open arms and trusted me alone in the archives with more than four decades of amazing scrapbooks and photos—you weren't kidding when you said you kept everything, and I'm so grateful you did.

Kurt, Kathy, Conner, Erin, and Jarrett, thank you for letting me barge into the Johnson family with my notepad and recorder to peer into your world. Your support was crucial.

I am fortunate to have stood on the shoulders of giants, not just in the composition of this book but in every aspect of my career. Thank you to my mentor, Phil Burgess, for hiring me to write for *National Dragster*. I hope this book makes you proud. Thank you to John Jodauga for taking me under your wing and sharing the Pro Stock beat with me, to Kevin and Jill McKenna for equal measures of insight and friendship, and to Brad Littlefield for being the one I could ask the most basic questions without feeling like I didn't belong. Brian Lohnes, my association with this project is because of you, and I will never forget it. I mean that in a good way.

Rick Voegelin and Bob Frey, the careful stats and notes that you compiled for various public sources provided structure to this book. Rick, your press materials were thorough, accurate, and informative, and your guidance was so very helpful. Mr. Frey, your lifelong labor of love in gathering and disseminating statistical information proved invaluable and unparalleled. I was able to tell a factual story through your contributions to DragRaceCentral.com in round-by-round notes and your "Did You Know?" columns.

I gathered a lot of information from printed material in Arlene's scrapbooks, so details from races and ideas for areas to delve into came from *National Dragster, Drag News, Drag Review, Motor Racing News,* the *Denver Post, Minneapolis Star Tribune,* and *"Drag News" from Minnesota Dragways.* Along with others mentioned, Larry Morgan, Linda Vaughn, Jerry Haas, Steve Burns, and Larry Olson each graciously spent time helping me put together a clear and accurate picture.

Many of the photos in this book were taken by Arlene Johnson. My sincere appreciation goes out to her for allowing me to use them. Boatloads of gratitude go out to Richard Shute and Auto Imagery, Steve Reyes, John Foster Jr., Keith Cyr, Evan Smith, Angel Ramos, Brandon Mudd, Randy Hennings and Ray-Mar Photos, Laura and Mark Bruederle, George Lieurance and the family of Les Welch, and Matt Levonas. Your images made this book beautiful.

The hours I devoted to this project were supported unwaveringly by my sweet family. Patrick, thank you for believing in me and cheering for me, especially in the early days when I was finding my way in the dark. Tori and Erin, thank you for the constant encouragement, plentiful hugs, baked goods, and reminders to take short breaks every hour. It worked!

To my editor, Wes Eisenschenk, thank you for your patience and guidance through this process, your support and wisdom when I was either dejected or excited, and most of all for trusting that I was the right person for the job.

You know, I always wanted to read a book about Warren Johnson. I just never thought I would be the one writing it. Enjoy.

INTRODUCTION

It seems silly to compose an introduction to a book about a legend, but you have this volume in your hands for a reason. You want to know more, and you will almost certainly find what you're looking for in the pages ahead.

Warren Johnson is one of the most well-known and decorated drag racers of all time. His brazen, take-no-bull, tell-it-like-it-is (even when it stings) attitude has been a breath of fresh air for some and wildly intimidating for others since day one. His approach to life, though, isn't what has made the history books.

No. 7 on the National Hot Rod Association's (NHRA) 50 Greatest Drivers list, Warren "the Professor" Johnson entered drag racing with an engineer's education. His first NHRA Pro Stock car was a brand spankin' new Camaro that he purchased in 1970, prepared for racing, and debuted at the U.S. Nationals. He nearly wore the car out, racing it as much as possible as he cemented the foundation for a fruitful, lifelong career both on and off the racetrack.

Warren Johnson has been inducted into the International Motorsports Hall of Fame, the NHRA Division 2 Hall of Fame, the Georgia Racing Hall of Fame, the Motorsports Hall of Fame of America, and the Don Garlits Museum of Drag Racing Hall of Fame, and he has been named as one of the Legends of Bristol Dragway. He was the second most winning professional driver in NHRA history at the time of this writing with 97 national event victories, and he owned a total of 8 championships (6 NHRA and 2 IHRA). He blasted to the first 200-mph run in NHRA competition and produced the power that sent his son, Kurt, to the Pro Stock category's first sub-7-second pass.

Age does not seem to be a factor for Warren because the seemingly tireless man was still building engines out of his Sugar Hill, Georgia, race shop while this book was under construction. He graciously stepped out of the engine room many times for the interviews that you will find here.

Warren Johnson is a man of few words, and that is mostly because he is hyperefficient, though precise, in all that he does. He doesn't believe in wasting time, and conversation without a purpose is just as invaluable as making a pass down the quarter mile with no intention of winning. He does not mince words, and his concise, meaningful expressions have been recorded in this book alongside all of the statistics and notes that tell the story of one of the most successful drag racers and engine builders of all time.

The photos alone, provided by some of the finest photographers the sport has ever seen, tell a delightful tale, and the contributions of Warren Johnson's friends, fellow racers, and family provide a well-rounded perspective of a racing life well lived.

Before the grandchildren were born, the Johnson family was a unit of four with son, Kurt, and his wife, Kathy.

CHAPTER 1

THE SEEDS OF SPEED

According to Warren Johnson (WJ), his unparalleled success in the arena of harnessing horsepower and generating speed boils down to two simple principles: hard work and resourcefulness. Most folks are capable of acquiring these attributes and refining them over time with thoughtful determination, but few have these traits as distinctly hardwired into the fiber of their being as "the Professor."

WJ's dedication to engine development, and ultimately to drag racing, produced 6 National Hot Rod Association (NHRA) championships and an enormous tally of 97 national event wins in the series—more than any other Pro Stock driver in the history of the sport at the time of this writing.

His achievements span beyond the confines of the NHRA though. WJ earned 2 Mountain Motor Pro Stock championships and 13 trophies over 5 years of competition in the IHRA, which he ran in conjunction with the full NHRA schedule for a time. WJ match raced relentlessly early in his career, earning cash and accolades in all sorts of drag racing arenas and shattering records across various sanctioning bodies.

WJ was 76 years old when these words were written, and at that time, he still seemed almost superhuman—or at the very least like a fellow who doesn't require a typical amount of sleep, vacation time, or even much of a lunch break. He and his wife, Arlene, were still arriving at Warren Johnson Enterprises at 7 a.m., working through the day, and locking up the shop 12 to 14 hours later to venture out for dinner. They did this every day of the week, and that had been their general routine for most of their adult lives.

Austere Beginnings

Warren Johnson was born in Virginia, Minnesota, to Howard and Edna on July 7, 1943. His brother, Clyde, was born two years later, and more than a decade later, their baby sister, Brenda, arrived.

The Johnson children grew up understanding that earning a living dictated the location and functionality of the family. For several years, they lived in Montana, where Howard worked in the Anaconda Copper Mine in Butte.

"My first memory was probably when we were living in West Yellowstone," said WJ. "It was winter in Montana, and you could just barely see the peaks of the roof of two-story houses. They tunneled underneath the snow on the streets using plows with augers, and I remember walking under the caverns of snow.

This is where it all began. Warren Johnson earned the first drag racing trophy of his career on May 5, 1963, in a '57 Chevy. WJ claimed, "That's the drug that started this disease." The inscription on the back of the photo by his wife, Arlene, reads: "Standing pretty proud with his trophy. Warren at the Minnesota Dragways, Mpls."

Arlene Johnson snapped this photo of her husband's first trial run in his C/Modified Production 1957 Chevrolet at Minnesota Dragways. Although WJ is well known as a GM campaigner, he said, "I'm not married to any brand. I'd race anything I could win with. I didn't care what it was, as long as I had the potential of winning."

Shoveling snow is a way of life in northern Minnesota. "You had to move that prefrozen water," said WJ. "And you had to know how to work on this kind of equipment in addition to using it. I worked on everything from hay bailers to plows. I grew up in a place that was 500 miles from where God left his shoes."

Growing up in the country meant being resourceful, but WJ is grateful for the education that came with working on all sorts of equipment. His experience as a self-taught welder landed him a position at Twin City Welding. The entity built tubular work (including back bumpers, elements of the skis, the steering section, and tie-rods) for every snowmobile manufacturer on the continent of North America.

"Before Montana, they tell me we lived in Chicago for a while and that I fell out of the second story of an apartment building there and landed on my head."

He paused, then grinned.

"Maybe that's what happened to me," he said.

After Montana, the family moved back home to Minnesota. His parents purchased a farm in Markham,

Knowledge-hungry WJ is shown in 1964, immersed in a manual. "My philosophy has always been that you can't solve a problem unless you understand it, and if you're going to understand, you have to bring in physics and chemistry and a bunch of stuff people don't normally think about," said WJ. "I've always taken the proverbial 'devil is in the details' approach."

approximately 30 miles from the town where WJ was born.

"I grew up in the country, and I wouldn't trade that for anything," he said. "You learned to be independent. As kids, my brother and I would cut pulp wood, trap weasels and beavers, and whatnot. I remember I got $35 for a mink one time, but I didn't trap it—I hit it with the car, knocked it out, and killed it with my hands.

"It was a different way of life, but I wouldn't trade growing up that way for a city life. If I had been raised in a city, I wouldn't have turned out the way I did. I'm not saying I turned out good, but I'm self-taught in everything I know how to do. That was how it had to be because you couldn't call someone if something broke. In fact, we never did have a telephone at the farm. You just fixed it yourself."

Both of WJ's parents worked outside of the home. Edna gathered samples in the iron-ore mines, and Howard traveled extensively as an international operating engineer. He zigzagged the globe, educat-

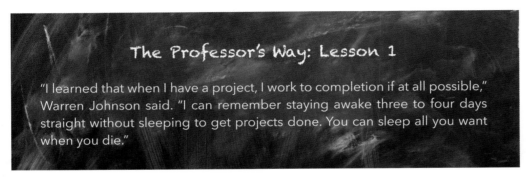

ing others in the operation of heavy-equipment shovels, Caterpillars, and earth movers. In WJ's early youth, his father was absent much of the year, venturing as far as Alaska, Australia, Venezuela, and Greenland.

"I was young enough that I didn't worry about where he was," said WJ with a shrug. "If I remember correctly, back then if you stayed overseas for 287 consecutive days, your income was tax-free. Being as frugal as we were, that was a no-brainer."

Frugality as a means of survival was the name of the game for the Johnson family in those early years, and that went hand in hand with taking care of what they

The '57 Chevrolet that WJ raced was also his daily driver. He purchased it from a used car lot, extracted the 283 Chevy small-block, and loaded it up with a 327 engine that he built himself. Here it is parked at the home of his in-laws during a visit in December 1963. Next to the Chevy is a 1958 Corvette that WJ had painted metal-flake blue for a friend, and in the background is a 1953 Jeep that belonged to Arlene's father. "It had a 4-cylinder in it and didn't have enough power to get out of its own way," said WJ. "I put a Chevy V-8 in it. I machined an adapter plate over at her uncle's so I could bolt a Jeep transmission to a Chevy engine."

had in order to eat. The task was large, and everyone was required to carry their share of the load.

"The farm was about 180 acres," said WJ. "It was pretty small compared to a lot of farms, but it was enough to raise crops and cows, chickens, and pigs. We were farm kids. We cut hay, bailed it, stored it, cleaned out the barn, and milked the cows. We learned that in order to survive, you had to work.

"I don't think we had a TV until maybe 1959, and then it was just a 13-inch black and white. We'd watch some cartoons and stuff, Pinky Lee, news that came out of Duluth 50 miles away. I think we just had one channel, and you'd watch whatever was on there. It didn't get very good reception, but we didn't watch much of it, anyway. There was work to be done."

Winter on the Iron Range was frigid, but life didn't pause or even slow down during the coldest months.

"The weather was a matter of perspective, really," said WJ. "It was just part of life. The coldest I ever remember was 52°F below zero, and that's without these fictitious windchills you hear about now. But you still went to work. I remember sitting in a sling welding steel in 30-below weather, just sitting there for eight hours burning rods. You learn to deal with it. It wakes your brain up, I guess you could say.

"But if you're at all cognizant, you don't want to do that all your life. You can't pick where you're born, but you can sure pick where you end up."

He concluded wryly, "I tell everyone who stays up there they have permafrost of the brain."

Defining a Career

"I wouldn't trade my parents for anyone else's," said WJ. "They were just regular people, but they were both very driven."

WJ undoubtedly absorbed his work ethic from the example of his parents, but his chosen application of the trait wasn't exactly embraced by both.

"My mother didn't care if we raced or worked on cars; whatever we wanted to do was fine with her, but my dad absolutely cared," WJ recalled. "He hated racing. He called it 'vehicle abuse,' and he wouldn't even go to the races. You have to remember, he lived through the Depression, when there was no money. I think the best way to explain it is to say that it seemed wasteful to him. He didn't understand that you could race for money. He just couldn't conceive of it."

Even without his father's nod of approval, WJ could not deny what piqued his interest most.

"Anything mechanical intrigued me," he said. "I became a self-taught welder and machinist. I never went to school for those things, I just learned them because they interested me. They still do. I probably delved into it a little further than someone who was learning from an instructor because I wanted to understand everything about it. Really learning to do these things allowed me to craft something that I wouldn't have been able to otherwise."

As was the theme throughout his childhood, skill was born from necessity for WJ. He began working on engines in the late 1940s and 1950s because, as he explained, the reliability of farm equipment and vehicles was inconsistent.

According to WJ, the life expectancy of a 6-cylinder Chevrolet engine at that time was approximately 30,000 miles due to the quality of lubricants, the iron block, and the rings. In the winter, he and his brother would overhaul farm equipment for others, building snowbanks

Warren and Arlene's son, Kurt, was born on March 23, 1963, one day short of the Johnsons' one-year wedding anniversary.

Kurt, age 3, with his dad after a long day in the body shop. WJ's own father, Howard, was often traveling for work when he was small, but Kurt was never far from his dad's side growing up. They raced together for many years and still work together.

Take a peek at the 1955 Chevy that WJ bought just out of high school.

"That was really the first car I had," said WJ of his '55 Chevy. "The engine in it when I bought it was a 302 Chevy, and I put in a 348 Chevy. I traded a '29 Ford roadster that I'd built with an Oldsmobile V-8 in it for the '55. If you notice, it doesn't have any door handles. Crazy kids."

The Professor's Way: Lesson 2

"I never considered that I was going out on a limb with my chosen career, but in retrospect, I guess it was sink or swim. I was only going to race as a job," Warren Johnson said. "That was first and foremost; it was how I was going to make a living. I honestly felt, after going to the University of Minnesota at night and looking at the average quality of engineers out there, that if these idiots could make a living doing something they didn't even seem to enjoy, I sure as hell could make a living doing something I liked.

"The thing I always remember is that most of them complained about the work they did. I always considered myself in the top 2 percent of the workforce because I enjoyed what I was doing. You're going to have good days or bad days in anything. Sometimes you can't solve something, things don't go the way you want, or you're not making enough money. But the easiest way to find a solution is to just look in the mirror. You'll usually see the problem."

Warren and Arlene took up residence in this home in Fridley, Minnesota, in 1969.

WJ's Competition Engine Service took up residence in the four-stall garage there.

WJ always said that an engine couldn't read the name on the hood. If the engine couldn't discriminate, neither could he. He applied this theory in the early 1970s, when he did some engine work and built transmissions for Midwest racer Vic Anderson's A/Fuel dragster. "It started out as an A/Gas dragster, then we put alcohol in it, then nitro," WJ said. "It was interesting to me."

around the project and tunneling underneath to get to work.

"I didn't see working in those conditions as a hardship; it was just what it took to get the job done," he said. "You didn't complain about it. You just did it."

The cold winter months brought the most challenging weather, and summer wasn't a time for rest or play. Work was year-round and nonstop for Johnson. From the time he was 12 years of age until he was 16, he worked for a high-end contractor from Duluth in the summertime, building and maintaining lake cabins for folks well outside of his own economical class.

In high school, WJ procured a position at Aurora Motor and Body Shop, overhauling vehicles and learning the basics in the trade of paint and bodywork. After graduation, when he was enrolled in junior college, WJ continued to learn and apply the trade at another body shop. Arlene, the bright-eyed, fun yet hardworking girl he married the year following high school graduation,

A strong work ethic was a necessity for WJ, whose duties as a young man included the operation of farm equipment to keep things running smoothly, particularly in Minnesota's cold winter months when snow needed clearing.

worked at a local bank. On the weekends, the newlyweds cleaned the body shop for $25 a week.

"It was a pretty good-sized shop, too," WJ said. "Probably about 80 feet wide by 150 feet long. Bodywork was a relatively dirty business with the dust and paint coming off the cars. It took a lot of sweeping to get that place clean, and we had to wash the floors down too. There couldn't be any dust in the building at the beginning of the week."

After attending junior college in Virginia, Minnesota, WJ enrolled in the University of Minnesota and moved to the Minneapolis area with Arlene. While there, he continued to hone his skills outside of the classroom. WJ welded ornamental iron and heavy steel for a shop that was looking to improve its product and make a profit. Once those goals were accomplished, he moved to a shop that primarily built tubing for snowmobiles.

WJ's fate was sealed, though, when he transitioned to running an automotive machine shop in the Minneapolis area. Perhaps it was a matter of being in the right place at the right time or maybe it was his characteristically effective calculation of a situation, but no matter the root cause, WJ's experience with that particular establishment set the trajectory for his career.

"They had some management problems in the warehouse, and that part of the business ended up going bankrupt," WJ explained. "The engine building part of the business was always profitable, but they couldn't run it themselves. So, I bought the equipment from them, added other equipment they didn't have, and started my own machine shop."

WJ's first shop of his own was a four-stall garage on the property of the home he and Arlene had moved to in Fridley, a northern Twin Cities suburb.

"I ran that for a number of years and was successful building road race, round track, and boat motors," he said. "I was pretty successful at anything I attacked, and that's kind of what led me to make the decision to race. I thought, if there is always racing going on, and I'm sup-

WJ has long been known as a relentlessly hard worker, tirelessly committed to the task at hand, whatever it may be. Here he is under the hood of his Chevy at the racetrack. "When you look at where we came from, failure was not an option," said WJ. "I was not going back."

The 1957 Chevy was painted a striking purple. Functioning as both a race car and the family vehicle, it was outfitted with a high-compression 327 engine. "I'd have to park it on a hill in the grocery lot so that I could get it going, and sometimes I'd have to have somebody help me push it," laughed Arlene. WJ shrugged and explained, "You just couldn't buy good starters back then."

plying successful engines, well, hell. I might as well go racing myself."

Taking the Wheel

As is true for many kids raised in a country setting, learning to drive wasn't restricted to the boundaries of the law for WJ and his siblings.

"You can see all the junk we used to have to haul with us to the racetrack," WJ said of this photo taken in 1963. "We'd drive the car up there with everything piled in the back seat and wherever we could fit it, change everything over, race it, change it back, then load everything back up so we could drive back. There was no such thing as a tow vehicle back then."

WJ works on the back half of his '57 Chevy.

"We didn't even have our driver's licenses when we learned to drive, but out in the country, who's going to stop you? We were driving farm equipment around out in the field, and nobody had a problem with that," said WJ. "Eventually, we realized it would be easier to drive on the road.

Jerry Korpela was along for the ride in the early days, accompanying WJ to the track for the first time in 1962 or so, said Arlene. WJ disputed the date. Here, Jerry and WJ pour gas into the 3-gallon tank at Minnesota Dragways in May 1963.

"That's the '40 Chevy," said WJ with the hint of a smile. "I built this '40. We actually dug it out of a snowbank, and I paid $40 for it. It was over at the house of a kid I went to school with. I saw it on the side of the road all the time, but I never thought anything of it until I started looking for something to build a race car out of."

"From the highway to where we lived, there was probably at least three or four miles of an all-gravel road. Between that and the ice and snow, that's probably where I learned car control. It's like walking. When you're first learning, it's really pretty difficult. But after that, it comes naturally. Then you know how to do it for the rest of your life."

WJ was 14 when he and his younger brother, Clyde, got hold of a 1949 Chevy.

"But we didn't like the way it looked, so we bought a '48. That's the one I really started playing with," he recalled. "The first new car I had was a 1966 Chevelle, a 396 4-speed. There were various cars through the years. I remember a '53 or '54 Chevy at one point in time, the

The First Crew Member

Arlene and Warren are shown in the mid-1960s, dressed up for a rare night out.

Arlene Johnson (yes, her maiden name was also Johnson) met WJ when they were seniors at different high schools. They were born just three days apart in 1943 (WJ on July 7 and Arlene on July 10), and although they didn't know it until many years later, their mothers went to school together. Arlene didn't know much about racing when she met WJ, but she was comfortable around it and open to being involved, largely because she had been the official parts washer and shop helper for her father, who did auto repair and engine work in the evenings and on the weekends. Although she did not accompany her husband on his first excursion as a spectator to the drag strip, Arlene was by his side every step of the way as he entered the world of acceleration and speed as a driver.

Arlene Johnson Q&A

Q: What did drag racing look like for you in the early days?

A: We'd go up to the track as a family. I had friends out there, and we all had little kids. As far as the cars going down the track, we really didn't know too much about them or pay attention. It was just a Sunday thing for us. We never thought it was going to come to this.

Q: Did you ever think about doing something else?

A: Not really. We got married in 1962, and I always worked. I worked at a bank, then a company that made industrial towel cabinets, then part time at a high-performance automotive warehouse in inventory, shipping, and receiving. In 1976, we started racing full time, and we did that for 38 years. It was just our way of life.

Q: Did you ever feel like it was a financial strain on the family?

A: From 1976 to 1982, we raced without a sponsor. But we did well enough because we could match race. We ran well, and Warren did all his own work, so we didn't have the high expenses of employees. It was just Warren, Kurt, and me.

Q: What were your duties in the early days?

A: Well, to start, I drove the truck and did at least half of the driving to the races and back. I always drove across Wisconsin when we left. Warren would have never made it to the track; when we would get to the Wisconsin state line, which was 35 miles, he would already be asleep. I would also pack the trucks, make sure we had food, and things like that.

Q: Did Kurt actually work too?

A: Oh, yes. He started working side by side with Warren when he was 12. Warren was patient, and still is to this day. I didn't have the patience. I was always more high-strung and would get frustrated.

Q: What was the biggest challenge in the beginning?

A: I think the biggest challenge was just getting everything ready and getting out of the door on time. We'd drive all night to get to the race the next morning.

Q: Did you enjoy it, though?

A: I did. It was hectic, but it was interesting, and it always kept you going. I still have that in me. I'm always in a hurry, even when I'm eating, I'm always rushing. We should have been retired 14 years ago, but we aren't ready for that.

"This is the first tunnel ram that I built for a small-block Chevy," WJ explained while examining the photo that he estimated was taken in 1963. "It was built out of steel because we didn't have any TIG welders up there to weld aluminum. I'm not kidding."

Loading up for Indy to race in A/Modified Production in 1968. "That was the time it let loose off the pickup," said WJ. "Someone else was hauling it for us. We were on the way to Indy in another car, maybe one or two vehicles behind. The car stayed on the trailer, but it went in the ditch and dented the fenders. We straightened them out at Indy. Those were just flesh wounds, no broken bones."

The resourceful WJ works on his race car in 1969 at the track using the flatbed trailer as a lift.

WJ won a trophy at Donnybrooke Speedway (Brainerd International Raceway) in 1969 and celebrated the victory with racing friends. From left to right are Herb Lang, Kathy Lang, Leroy Venne, Arlene, Kurt, WJ, Chuck Albers, and an unidentified friend.

A group gathered around WJ before he made a pass at Minnesota Dragways in 1968. Greg Jones, far right, contributed to Johnson's racing operation in the very early days.

In the 1960s, WJ was a regular at dragstrips in the surrounding area, including Interstate Dragways in Moorhead, Minnesota, and Minnesota Dragways (shown) in Coon Rapids, Minnesota.

WJ's first real race car, shown at the drag strip in Indianapolis in 1968, was this A/Modified Production 1940 Chevy. WJ recalled, "This is one of the first times we went to Indy for class eliminations. We probably ran that car three or four years. When I bought the '70 Camaro to race in Pro Stock, I drove it home from the dealership in northern Minnesota, stripped it, took the motor out of it, and put it in the '40 Chevy to sell it."

WJ accepts the trophy for his A/Modified Production win in 1969 at Donnybrooke, now known as Brainerd International Raceway.

Oh, there was more than a trophy for WJ when he raced to victory at Donnybrooke in July 1969 in his A/Modified Production '40 Chevy. He also claimed a check for $350.

'40 Chevy that we raced in A/Modified Production, and of course the '57 Chevy.

"That's the one [the '57] I drove to the racetrack, raced, and drove back. I think about it now, doing that with the spindly components. I carried rear axles and all that because I had to be back to work on Monday morning, and the racetrack was 200 miles away. Back then, that was far. That was my work car too, and Arlene drove it to the grocery store. It was the only car we had."

The multipurpose Chevrolet carried Johnson to his first final round, which took place at an NHRA division race at Minnesota Dragways in the early 1960s. There, he was runner-up to Minneapolis-based Jim Lutz. The noted Lutz and Lundberg team was the A/Gas record holder at the time, but that previously established acclaim didn't soothe the sting for WJ.

"That's when I learned that losing really sucks," he said as he shook his head, leaned back in his office chair, and crossed his arms.

The Professor's Way: Lesson 3

"Going faster is simply a case of making everything more efficient, and that's always been my approach to racing," Warren Johnson said. "It's all about making the vehicle, engine, and everything in the car more efficient. A race engine has to be as efficient as possible. You're only going to get so much energy out of the gasoline that you put into it, so you have to figure out how to burn it as efficiently as possible."

CHAPTER 2

FAMILY MATTERS

Warren Johnson's commitment to full-time racing was never a solo venture. He was married and now had a young son, so the decision would shape more than just one man's future. It set in motion a lifestyle for his family that would revolve, indefinitely, around Pro Stock.

Arlene and WJ had both accepted and lived within their financial means, and they worked as a team to support racing as a part-time gig. When WJ decided to go all in, he didn't get an outward argument from his wife.

"She went along with it. That must have meant she condoned it, at least to some extent," he said. "I'm a driven person by nature. I was not going to fail. She knew."

In It Together

Without personally knowing Arlene Johnson, one might assume that a woman who would go along agreeably with such a decision is a quiet, docile creature who is likely just bowing to her husband's wishes. That assumption could not be further from the truth.

"I went along with it because I was always interested in cars," Arlene said.

She leaned in conspiratorially and continued, "But he's able to do what he likes to do, and I can do anything I want to do. He never questions it. We haven't ever really been dependent on each other, but we've always worked together. Whether that's good or bad, I don't know. But it's worked so far."

The Professor's Way: Lesson 4

"I don't care what vocation you choose; you have to make sacrifices if you're going to be successful," Warren Johnson said. "I don't know of anyone in any avenue of employment that hasn't had to make a lot of sacrifices to be as good as they want to be. God didn't give any of us enough talent to be the best in the world right off the bat. You're the sole determiner of how good you will be."

Anecdotes from the Archive

With racing as the main focus in their world, priorities in the Johnson household were somewhat skewed when held against those of non-racing families. Eyebrows were often raised when folks outside of the business got a glimpse behind the scenes.

"The landlord came in at one point to paint our house and put down new carpet, and when we pushed the bed over, there were all of these race car parts underneath," recalled Arlene.

"They were cylinder heads," laughed WJ.

Arlene nodded in agreement before continuing, "The landlord said, 'You're not going to put those on the new carpet, are you?' I told him that those parts were cleaner than the new carpet would be," she said, seemingly bewildered and perhaps a bit offended by the question.

Life in the Johnson household allowed Kurt to begin learning the ins and outs of the automotive industry at a very young age.

When Kurt was a baby and WJ and Arlene would go racing for the weekend, Warren's parents, Edna and Howard, would care for him.

Kurt with his grandparents in 1966.

The Johnson family is shown just a handful of months after Kurt was born on March 23, 1963. This photo was taken outside of the small basement apartment that the little family called home in Virginia, Minnesota.

Arlene, WJ, and Kurt are all dressed up in 1967.

The two met after a dance in their late teens while still in high school.

"My cousin and I needed a ride home, and she said, 'I know Warren and Frankie; we can ride home with them,'" recalled Arlene. "So, we rode home, and the next thing was New Year's Eve, and they asked us if we wanted to go out with them. It went from there."

The early conversations between Warren and Arlene revealed a common interest: cars. Arlene had a bit of an unusual upbringing for a female at that time because she helped her father work on engines and was the official parts cleaner. She related to the appeal of engines and automobiles.

"When I met Warren, he had a fast car," Arlene said. "I don't think that was what attracted me to him, but that could have been part of it. It just seemed like we hit it off. Probably because I knew more about things like that than some of the other girls."

Warren and Arlene married on March 24, 1962. One day short of their one-year wedding anniversary, Kurt (KJ) was born.

Although she knew about cars, Arlene admitted that she didn't know a thing about racing. In the beginning, racing as a family meant that they would go to the track together. Warren and his friends worked on the cars and raced, and the wives minded the children, fed the group, and kept the coolers stocked.

Little Kurt (KJ) is tuckered out and resting with the family dog after a full day.

Even as a small child, Kurt was always by his father's side, watching him work and helping him as he grew old enough to do so. "He had an accelerated learning curve working with me," said WJ. "I was able to teach him what I had taught myself from machining to welding and what-not. Kurt has always had a natural physical aptitude for anything mechanical. He can figure out a lot of stuff, and I don't even have to show him."

It didn't make a bit of difference to Kurt where his dad was racing. He happily rode along in the back of the truck, where he had bunk space and could watch over the shoulders of his parents as they rode down the highway to the next race.

The life of a race car driver wasn't all glamorous. Here, WJ kills time shelling walnuts by the road-side when the box truck broke down on the way home from an event.

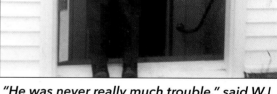

A little downtime after hours brings the racetrack into the family living room. Dick Smallwood (center) and his wife, Lori, lived across the fourplex from the Johnsons in Minneapolis.

"He was never really much trouble," said WJ of son KJ, shown here in 1967.

Growing up without a sibling wasn't too difficult for Kurt. He had friends like Ritchie Erickson to hang out with at the racetrack. This photo was taken by Arlene in 1968.

KJ (right) poses for a photo with Arlene's brother, Kenny. Born just three months apart, the two grew up together between the farm where Arlene's mother lived and the Johnson household.

Arlene is by the side of the Oldsmobile Cutlass with her video camera. Early on, she helped her husband's car through the burnout, pushing on the rear side panel to keep it in the waterbox. Later, she took over photo and video duties, filming and cataloging every run for WJ to go over. (Photo Courtesy Auto Imagery)

Although he was intensely focused on racing and often took much criticism from those outside who thought him surly, WJ truly enjoyed his family. When the annual race at Brainerd International Raceway came around, he and Arlene were afforded the opportunity to spend time with their extended families and friends. This photo of WJ with his niece, Brianna Oseland, was taken in 1986 at the Northstar Nationals.

In a true testament to the all-hands-on-deck nature of the operation, KJ's wife, Kathy, and Arlene pack the parachutes after a run.

Kurt and WJ discuss the upcoming run over the top of the race car. "He always worked with me in the shop in Minnesota," said WJ. "One day, he was feeling a little frisky and told me, you know, there are child labor laws. I said, 'Not here.'"

"The moms and kids would get together and watch when the guys raced, but I didn't have a clue as to what was going on," said Arlene. "It was just something fun to do, but it kept growing from there, more and more each year.

"When he decided to race full time, it was like, 'Okay, do you know what you're doing?' He was racing against Jenkins, Sox & Martin, Dick Landy, Bill Bagshaw—big names. It didn't bother him a bit. He was going to do it, so that's what we did."

Traditional households were run quite differently then, but rather than finding isolation in her unique sit-uation, Arlene thrived on friendships she formed within the racing community. Fairly quickly, she also found her way to being an indispensable part of the race team. Meals—and later, her famous margaritas—were only a small part of the responsibilities that she claimed along the way.

"I would do whatever needed to be done," she said in a Mother's Day article for DragRaceCentral.com in 2011. "When Kurt was little and Warren and I were racing, it was basically the three of us. I changed tires, charged the batteries, fueled it up, changed jets in the carburetors, packed the parachutes. I didn't do

WJ and Arlene visit with friends inside the race trailer after a full day's work in 1992.

Always a dog lover, Arlene and Bailey, Wally Clark's pup, spend some quality time together at the track in Montreal at Le GrandNational in 1992.

anything major, but I helped with the little things so that Warren could take care of whatever else needed to be handled. I was involved with it enough to keep me busy and not get bored, and it was a learning experience for me."

Later, when the racing program grew to include a hired crew, Arlene's role shifted some. She traveled with the crew in the truck from race to race, relinquishing some of her duties on the race car and increasing her role as "mom" to the guys on the team. Back at the race shop, Arlene managed all of the office duties, including payroll, employee paperwork, shipping and receiving, and of course, making sure everyone was fed.

The degree of dedication required for their lifestyle wouldn't have worked for everyone, but racing together was something that Arlene deemed a positive environment to raise a family.

"It was good for us," she said. "We traveled and got to see a lot of the country. Most people haven't been out of the area where they grew up, but we traveled north and south, east and west, on just about every road you could travel on. We did everything as a family. I think it was good for all of us."

Growing up Johnson

WJ didn't have a preference as to whether or not his child would be a boy or a girl, he said, but he also jokingly claimed that he told Arlene, "If it's a girl, we could just trade with somebody."

No trades were necessary when their son, Kurt, was born on March 23, 1963.

From a very early age, KJ took interest in what his father was doing in the shop. According to Arlene, the two were side by side from the time KJ was little. There was no forced education for KJ; he was genuinely interested in learning and being part of the process.

"Kurt has enough aptitude and brainpower that he could have done whatever he wanted to do; that opportunity was there from day one," said WJ. "Had he decided he didn't want to be involved in racing, I would have been more than happy to help in another endeavor."

But WJ's only offspring instinctively followed in his footsteps and was just as intrigued by mechanics and engineering as his father. KJ's early memories center around being in the garage watching, learning, and doing.

WJ stands with Arlene's brother, Kenny Johnson, in the pit area in Brainerd in 1991.

"I liked it. I'm sure it would have been different if I had brothers or sisters and wandered off to do something with them, but I was solo," said KJ. "It gave me something to do. Even if I was at my grandma's house, my uncle [Arlene's brother, Kenny] was only three months older than me, and we were always in the garage. I've been doing this all my life."

KJ tried his hand at baseball and enjoyed being part of the swim team. Although he claims he was probably wide enough (Mom has always been a good cook), he wasn't quite right for football.

WJ didn't recall Kurt being much trouble as a kid, but he was a normal teenager. KJ admits that he "partied like hell" in high school.

"Oh, he'd be late coming home sometimes, but when he did, he caught the wrath of Arlene," said WJ with a chuckle. "I'm always a little bit laid back with that kind of stuff. I knew what I used to do, so I fully expected him to be somewhat the same. But he never really got into too much trouble, and he maintained good grades. He had to maintain an A average if he wanted to go to the races."

And KJ very much wanted to go racing, so he kept up his grades, toed the line (a reasonable amount of the time for a teen), and maintained a level of shared respect with his parents.

The relationship between KJ and WJ was greatly enhanced from the beginning by two very important factors. First was Kurt's natural aptitude for anything mechanical, as his father explained. Second was the method of communication between the two.

The Professor's Way: Lesson 6

"I don't think Kurt and I honestly had any real serious disagreements, but we've never had words about anything because both of us are low-key enough that we think through the problem," Warren Johnson said. "If you're wrong, you admit it. If you're right, you try to convince the other one, but I don't think we've ever had a cross word. Ever."

"Kurt and I have gone days on end without saying a word to each other," said WJ. "We have enough confidence in each other's work that we don't have to go back and check it. We know the task at hand, both of us have our areas we work in, and at the end of the day it all comes together. Talking for no reason is something politicians do. It's just a waste of time."

Throughout his youth, Kurt earned his keep and continued his hands-on education working on the race car, tearing apart transmissions, helping to assemble engines, and doing anything else required.

"He had the ability to do it all because he'd been around it from knee-high to a grasshopper, as they say," said WJ. "He was good at everything, but especially deductive reasoning. For most people, thinking is too hard of work. It sounds like manual labor to them. But Kurt was always good at that. He'd see something happen and could pretty well deduce why, and he could always figure out how to circumvent a problem."

Kenny Johnson, Arlene's brother, with KJ at a race in the mid-1990s. Kenny and KJ were good friends growing up.

CHAPTER 3

A NEW CLASS

In 1970, a new class was born in NHRA competition. Pro Stock caught Warren Johnson's attention rather quickly.

"It was the mechanical challenge of it more than anything else," he explained. "But it was also something I felt I could make a decent living at if I did it well. I guess I looked at it from the perspective of an investor: they know they aren't going to make a million their first day; they had to learn how to invest. It's the same thing in racing. I didn't know anything about it, other than the object was to win. A lot of education went into learning how to win and then making it a business."

Once he set his sights on Pro Stock, WJ moved swiftly to secure his future. He settled on a brand-new Chevrolet Camaro, and there were only a few available in his home state at that time. He found his at the Martin Chevrolet dealership in Virginia, Minnesota, the town three and a half hours away in which he was born and raised.

The 1972 version of WJ's Chevy Camaro was self-titled. (Photo Courtesy John Foster)

"I had some experience with the big-block Chevy because that's what I'd run in the A/Modified Production car," WJ explained of his selection. "Being that you had to use a corporate engine in any car you ran, deductive reasoning made the Camaro an obvious choice. So, I went to the dealership and bought a new one, drove it the 200 miles home, stripped it, and started turning it into a Pro Stock car."

Since the early days of his career, WJ has broken down drag racing and horsepower in simple terms to achieve results. "This isn't rocket science," he said. "It's racing for 1,320 feet. There's only so much that can happen in a quarter of a mile."

The Professor (pictured here in 1970) has always kept a keen eye on the future and what's next in the world of drag racing. "Drag racing is an engineering exercise in its purest form–you either win or lose," said WJ.

In May 1970, WJ was informed that he couldn't run without a hood scoop at a local track. Short on materials, he scoured the area, found a cardboard beer box, and quickly "fabricated" one.

Initial Investment

Although he cannot recall exactly how much he paid for it, WJ recalled that the purchase price of his new Camaro landed somewhere between $2,200 and $2,300. That amount is small by today's standards, but in 1970 and for a notoriously frugal gentleman, that was a large chunk of change.

WJ's first Pro Stock Camaro takes a trip down the quarter mile in 1970.

"I basically don't pay a whole lot of attention to the rules anyway," said WJ. "We didn't have anything else, so I fabricated the required hood scoop using what I could. It was a testament to duct tape."

"I knew this wasn't going to be an 'overnight sensation' deal," he said of the expense. "I was making an investment in racing—that's really what it amounted to—so I didn't look at the cost as being that much. Of course, it was a lot of money at that time, especially when you're

WJ is in the staging lanes in 1970 waiting to make a run. The attire of the day for a drag racer? Just what one would expect: sneakers, trousers with a shop rag in the back pocket, and a short-sleeved, button-down shirt.

This is what the pits looked like in 1970.

WJ installed a roll bar in his Camaro in February 1971. The back of this photo from the family archives is labeled "Progress."

WJ's Chevrolet Camaro underwent extensive changes in preparation for racing in 1971, many of which took place inside of his four-bay garage in Fridley, Minnesota.

The Chevy is reassembled after upgrades and waiting for paint.

Rain or shine, WJ was working on his program. Snow on the ground didn't make a bit of difference the day they sent the Camaro off to get a fresh coat of paint before the new season.

working for $1.39 an hour as a welder, plus attending the University of Minnesota. But being from northern Minnesota, you're naturally pretty frugal. Arlene and I had saved as much as we could out of both of our incomes, so we were able to pay for it in cash."

The first thing he did was remove the barely used small-block that was in the heart of his soon-to-be Pro Stocker and drop it into his old 1940 Chevy, which he then sold to offset costs. The big-block in his former race car went into the Camaro, and WJ set to work preparing his new hot rod for competition.

Although WJ was never too concerned with aesthetics over performance, he had some fine-looking race cars. Here's his early Camaro getting a fresh coat of paint before the new lettering was applied.

The first major aesthetic change for WJ's Chevrolet Camaro was a splash of fresh, vibrant color. It was painted a rich red tone in March 1971.

The Professor's Way: Lesson 7

In what little spare time he had, Warren Johnson built engines in his four-stall garage in Fridley, Minnesota. The small side business created an avenue to supplement his meager welder's income and keep his racing going, but he never actively pursued customers. All of his business came from word of mouth, and his ever-developing expertise in the field of high performance was sought from multiple motorsports platforms, including circle track, sports car, and boat racing.

"I didn't advertise, but people came to me. I think a lot of my education came easy to me because I'm a good listener," he said with a grin over his steady gaze. "I don't really talk a whole lot, but I listen. I process information and utilize what I perceive as being useful. That's the way I've been all my life."

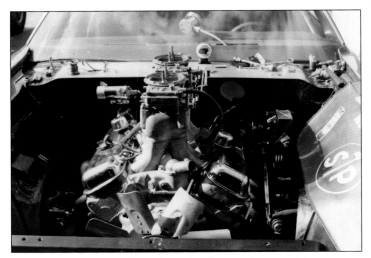

A closer look at the handiwork of WJ's Competition Engine Service Inc. in his Camaro in June 1971.

"I built this tunnel ram for a big-block in 1965, way before anyone else came out with a tunnel ram," said WJ in reference to the performance-enhancing double-carburetor intake system.

The scenic pit area of Minnesota's Donnybrooke Speedway, which later became Brainerd International Raceway, offered shady trees as covering for maintenance between passes. WJ got to work changing a gear in the transmission in this shot taken in July 1971.

WJ and friends are shown around the engine compartment of his Camaro on a day he raced John Hagen three times and won all at Minnesota Dragways in August 1971.

The Camaro displays Competition Engine Service, Inc. branding in 1971. (Photo Courtesy John Foster)

A look inside the engine compartment in July 1971 at Minnesota Dragways.

On the back of this photo, Arlene inscribed: "Lettering just finished on Camaro. Early spring 1971."

WJ put many miles on his first Camaro, shown here with the 1971 paint scheme and a hood scoop that had undergone some fabrication as he worked to find the most efficient means of harnessing horsepower. (Photo Courtesy John Foster)

When completed, the aluminum-headed 427-ci big-block Chevy was complemented by a tunnel ram intake manifold and dual 660-cfm Holley 4-barrel carburetors. With his four-stall garage in Fridley as his workshop, WJ devoted every free moment to the project, and the "free" moments were few and far between.

"If I remember right, it took two or three months to get everything ready," he said. "At that point in time, the tube chassis hadn't even been thought of, so you just used the basic car itself. I don't think you could use fiberglass doors or fenders yet either. It had to be a stock Camaro other than the big-block that was in it, but I was working full time and going to school part time, so that didn't leave a whole lot of hours in the day."

Once the parts and pieces were in place with his first Pro Stock car, the education really began. WJ's initial goal set the tone for a lifetime of successful racing. It was just a case of figuring out how to get his race car to stay pointed straight down the track and run respectably. With what WJ claims is "nine months of winter and three months of tough sledding," the window of opportunity for racing in his home state was very narrow. But true to form, WJ was efficient. In that first tight timeframe of a season, he wrenched his way from clocking 10-second passes down the quarter mile into the 9s.

Establishing the performance criteria for his combination boiled down to feeling his way through every pass down the racetrack. WJ navigated the accelerated learning curve as he dialed in the engine, chassis, and driveline simultaneously and laid the foundation for nearly five decades of a life dedicated to success in the Pro Stock class.

Staying in His Own Lane

The first trip to the racetrack with the Camaro revealed all of its weak spots, but it wasn't a painful lesson for the Professor. It only served to help steer the ship.

"I knew right away that we better get to work if we were going to get this thing up on speed and performance," WJ said. "There were no pro chassis builders at that point in time, so you built what you thought was right, and you had to prove to yourself whether what you did was right or wrong.

"That's why you brought cutters and welders with you to the racetrack. We'd do whatever we thought we needed in order to fix something. A lot of that was redundant work, but when you're learning, if 50 percent of what you do is right, you're way ahead of the game. Usually, about 10 percent of what you do is right. It was all just part of the learning curve. It was the college education of drag racing."

En Route to the NHRA

WJ was a regular on the United Drag Racers Association (UDRA) circuit in the dawn of his Pro Stock career. The UDRA, established in 1964, was born in Southern California but later moved its home base to the

A moment captured in 1970 on an evening after racing all day. WJ is wearing the hat of his buddy, Greg Jones, while having a beer.

The Professor's Way: Lesson 8

Perhaps one of the greatest keys to Warren Johnson's unparalleled career success is that he didn't typically give his opponent much thought when it came down to his plan of attack on any given run at any given race. Although, he did get a kick out of raising ire in his competitors on occasion with some fairly epic staging duels.

"I honestly don't pay a lot of attention to other people," WJ said with a shrug. "I just concentrate on my own program. When I race, I know that I can only take care of my own lane; I don't have enough brain power to worry about two of them.

"In the early days, I couldn't even tell you if there was anybody else out there. We were concentrating on getting everything together and working on our performance at the same time. We were totally engrossed in our car, and we weren't worried about anybody else. With most things, that's how it should be."

WJ's 1971 race schedule included events at Sioux City, Iowa. The family loaded up the Camaro on its flatbed truck and headed that way on May 22, 1971.

Paul Marcotte and WJ over the engine compartment prepare for another pass at Amber Green Dragways in Eau Claire, Wisconsin, in June 1971.

Danny Lappi created this poster for WJ in 1971.

The Competition Engine Service, Inc.-branded Camaro launches at Minnesota Dragways in 1971. (Photo Courtesy John Foster Jr.)

A good time was had by all. The crew at Sioux City, Iowa, on May 23, 1971.

weren't like they are today, where you have to change valve springs every run.

"The valvetrain was really not an issue as far as reliability. The valve springs would basically be in there for months at a time. You never had a problem with them, even though the quality wasn't as good as it is today. Back then, though, you were only making 800 hp."

The UDRA was a pleasing and lucrative venture for WJ, but racing in the series wasn't exactly a cakewalk. Less-than-ideal track conditions demanded active participation from drivers who, out of necessity, became acutely in tune with their race cars. That was just fine for WJ. It was just another level of education, and in a publicity interview with General Motors in 2001, he referred to his time racing the UDRA series as some of his "best driver training."

Midwest. In 1970, the same year Pro Stock was recognized as an official NHRA category, UDRA launched its own Pro Stock circuit.

Joined by the likes of Wayne Gapp, Jack Roush, and Joe Satmary, WJ enjoyed the UDRA program and found it fairly lucrative.

"If you had to travel over 500 miles, you made sure they had two races at the facility for the weekend—that way, you could at least break even," he recalled. "I ran a lot of those races. It was a pretty good gig for us, and if we ran well enough, we could make money at it. Of course, back then the cars were pretty low maintenance. They

The NHRA was another sector that WJ saw as potentially viable, and he scheduled his National Hot Rod Association debut for the 1971 U.S. Nationals. Indy was the most prestigious event on the NHRA schedule and one that brought more cars to the starting line than any other drag race in the country.

"Oh no, I wasn't nervous," said WJ with a shake of the head when asked. "Nervousness is usually the result of a lack of preparation, and being nervous is nothing but a waste of time and energy anyway. But I wouldn't say I

Here's a look at what was beneath the hood of WJ's Chevrolet Camaro when he ran it at Minnesota Dragways. The 427 is outfitted with an Edelbrock manifold and Holley 4500 carburetors with velocity stacks.

WJ talks carburetors with Ed Hecht from Holley at Indy in 1971. WJ was hungry for knowledge from the very beginning. For the Professor, correct application of acquired knowledge translated to horsepower and, ultimately, victory.

The Professor's Way: Lesson 9

Warren Johnson's self-assurance has sometimes been misconstrued as an over-inflated ego, but it really comes down to believing to his core that no one person is better than another by nature.

"I never looked at the competition and considered them any better than I was," he said. "I've never really been intimidated by anyone because we're all born with challenges and abilities. It comes down to problem solving. When you're presented with a situation, you have to analyze it. You can't solve a problem unless you understand it, so it starts there. If the problem is performance, you just keep working at it until it's where you need it to be."

Although this ideology speaks to his ability to run with the big dogs before he was ready to properly bark, it has also generated frustration for WJ throughout his career. It's a tough pill for the Professor to swallow when he sees others not living up to their potential.

"Successful racing is like any business: you take care of what you have to in order to make it successful," he said.

A lot of effort went into preparing for the 1971 U.S. Nationals. WJ took a few moments for a quick snooze while waiting to go through tech. That's good friend Kathy Lang, who traveled with her husband, Herb, to many events with the Johnsons.

was overly confident either. Back then, you had all the Mopar factory teams and whatnot, and I was just some schmuck from up in the Northwoods. By anyone else's standards, I shouldn't have been there in the first place, but I figured that they put their pants on the same way I do."

Once they were on-site at what was then known as Indianapolis Raceway Park, WJ and Arlene settled in for the weekend with fellow Minnesota racers in the campground. They pitched tents that served as functional and reasonably priced accommodations.

WJ's first NHRA event and U.S. Nationals debut yielded less-than-stellar results. WJ qualified No. 28 in the 32-car field and was ousted in the first round by Don Grotheer. But the "schmuck" from up in the Northwoods had his foot in the door and was quickly learning the territory.

Racing was hard work, and WJ never took that part lightly, but he also knew when and where to log downtime for a meal or a conversation. Here he is (middle) in the pits at his first NHRA event with friends Herb Lang (left) and Bill Judnick.

Indy Highlights

Throughout his career, WJ logged many standout moments at the U.S. Nationals and the NHRA's venerable drag strip nestled on the outskirts of one of the most noted cities in American motorsports.

His first Indy win came in 1984, when WJ was driving the 1984 Oldsmobile Cutlass he somewhat affectionally refers to as the *Flying Boxcar*. The Olds had virtually no downforce in the rear.

"It felt like you were driving in the rain every time you went down the track," said WJ.

The win was particularly memorable, as it came with a final-round defeat of Indiana native and archrival Bob Glidden, who already had five U.S. Nationals trophies on the mantel at the time.

Nearly a decade later, as the defending event champ in 1993 and in the midst of an intense rivalry with the Dodge Boys, WJ scored a third win in Indianapolis. This time it was over Mopar campaigner Scott Geoffrion. The history between the two was ever-palpable on the starting line. Geoffrion began his Pro Stock career as a team driver for WJ in 1991, before he and Darrell Alderman became Mopar teammates.

That day at the U.S. Nationals, the energy between WJ and his longtime friend-turned-competitor was off the charts, and at the finish-line stripe, the margin of victory was just 0.001 second. WJ later named the win as one of his most rewarding because of the "questionable performance enhancements" suspected to be employed by those particular competitors at the time.

In all, WJ won the U.S. Nationals six times (1984, 1992, 1993, 1994, 1995, and 1999). At the time of his departure from driving in 2014, only one Pro Stock racer (nine-time Indy winner Bob Glidden) had more success at drag racing's most historic event.

This is what tech inspection looked like in 1971 at the U.S. Nationals.

"That first trip to Indy was part of the learning curve," said WJ. "I've said it before. You have to learn how to race, and you have to learn what you need to do to win. I wasn't a crew chief for somebody for a dozen years, so I had to learn everything about the racing business at my own expense. That first race at Indy was just part of the process."

For those fortunate to be part of the U.S. Nationals in its heyday, an impression was made that sometimes set the bar unreasonably high. The impact of WJ's first Indy experience was lasting, although he didn't enter that first NHRA event with exorbitant expectations.

"It was just another place to race for me," he said. "I wasn't evaluating sanctioning bodies or anything like that; I was just looking for new places to race. Having never been there before, I didn't know what to expect. I may have read about it here or there, but in reality, it was just one of the closer venues for me, and it fit my schedule.

WJ and his Camaro match raced frequently at Minnesota Dragways. Here he is burning some rubber in 1972. (Photo Courtesy John Foster Jr.)

The Johnson family hauled its race car on a flatbed trailer in the early days like most racers at the time. This gave the folks on the highway an up-close view of the Camaro with that shiny gold Warren Johnson lettering on the side.

WJ's Camaro gets some attention after a 9.59-second pass that came with a broken rear end. Parking lots made fine work spaces while on the road. The photo was taken in Van Wert, Ohio, in 1972.

"The only thing that really sticks out in my mind is the sheer volume of competitors in all categories. I remember having 1,500 competitors at this event, now we see maybe 700 or so. But back then, it was a lot more affordable to dabble in drag racing. Travel didn't cost near what it does today, and very few people had tractor trailers or big setups like that. People would haul on flatbed trailers, and there were a few enclosed trucks and a lot of box trailers. It was just more economical to race then."

The Right Fit

WJ knew that Pro Stock was where he wanted to be. However, after that initial run at the NHRA competition, he was well aware that he had some work to do if he was going to gain measurable success.

For the remainder of 1971 and on through 1975, he laid more groundwork as a driver, engine builder, and tuner on the match racing and AHRA circuits. WJ also continued his formal education and dedicated time to growing his engine-building business, and he steadily moved forward.

"The development end of things is what has always intrigued me," he said. "Gasoline and carburetors fit right into my wheelhouse. I had no love of Fuel cars at that point and thought of them as mechanical masochists. If you're going to race and hope to make a profit, you have to look at a category that fits your interests. Otherwise, it's going to become a real job and a real drag, so to speak."

The ground-up build is shown for WJ's new Vega, which he predicted would punch a smaller, more-efficient hole through the air as it raced down the track.

The Vega

In 1975, the engineer in WJ hit upon an idea.

"I was looking solely at aerodynamics, and I figured that if you punch a smaller hole, you'll go through the air easier, even if the car isn't aerodynamically shaped," he said. "The Chevy Vega fit that idea pretty well."

WJ enlisted the help of a builder named George Wepplo, who crafted the car from the ground up with his direction.

WJ took on the AHRA Pro Stock competition and Competition Eliminator's B/A class in the NHRA with this tidy little Vega. It was a handful, but WJ said he enjoyed wheeling it because it gave him "plenty to do." (Photo Courtesy Auto Imagery)

This shows early stages of construction for the Vega, an all-tube, double frame-rail car constructed of 4130 alloy. "George Wepplo was an excellent fabricator, equally as good as Don Ness," said WJ. "I outlined everything I wanted on the car. Instead of struts, it had a regular A-arm front suspension, and George custom-made everything."

Warren and Arlene hauled the Vega home for the first time on June 22, 1973.

"It was completely built out of just body panels and tubing," WJ recalled. "There was no regular vehicle to start with. I was working full time and still going to school, so I didn't have time to build a car, but George was an excellent fabricator. This was about the time Don Ness was starting to build cars, and I might have commissioned him if I had known him. But, George did an excellent job."

Although some have debated the fact—and with arguable evidence—WJ stands firm in his statement that the Vega was stable. Weighing in at right around 1,800 pounds and built more like a road race vehicle than a drag car, the little Chevy was a prime example of WJ's infatuation with innovation. It was a double frame-rail control-arm car that had custom-fabricated spindles and no front struts. The big-block and manual 4-speed combination produced 8.6-second passes at 160 mph.

"It was a good driver-training car. That's what it amounted to," said WJ, who went on to explain that he was prepared to pilot challenging vehicles before his formal drag racing career even started.

"Without a doubt, having been from northern Minnesota and driving on ice and snow, you learn car control in a way that most people don't. A drag racing car is spinning the tires continuously from one end of the track to the other; it's like driving a car 150 mph in the rain. But if you're used to that type of behavior from a vehicle, it's not really that difficult."

The Chevy Vega is getting decked out with a proper engine and components. "That was a really good car to drive," said WJ. "That's when I ran that small-cubic-inch big-block, 383 inches, with a manual 4-speed. It ran 8.60s at 160-plus mph."

The body is midway through the painting process. When the car was finally ready, WJ primarily raced it in the AHRA because the "big-block in a Vega" combination didn't fit the NHRA's rules. "It was a good car for match racing, and it fit in well in [the] AHRA," said WJ. "I ran the hell out of that thing."

The Vega is fresh from getting a paint job conceptualized and applied by Bruce "Peanuts" Mayhre of N.E. Auto Body. WJ explained that Peanuts offered to paint it, and he gave him free rein in terms of design. "I wasn't planning to take it to a car show anyway," said WJ. "All I wanted to do was race the thing."

The Vega wasn't legal for Pro Stock at that time other than in AHRA competition, so WJ got additional seat time racing it in the NHRA B/Altered category.

In all, WJ campaigned the car for about a year and a half before selling it. According to legend, the next owner swapped the engine for a small-block, crashed it on the first pass, and lost the use of his left arm. It is said that the Vega found its final resting place in a hole in the desert, where it was buried after the crash.

Although WJ thrived on the creativity involved in the process of building the Vega from the ground up, and almost begrudgingly admits that the challenge of driving the car had "somewhat of a fun factor," it doesn't rank among his favorites. In fact, none of his race cars do.

"The Vega was way ahead of its time. But to me, a Pro Stock car was nothing but a 9/16 wrench, the most common in the toolbox," he stated simply. "It was a weapon that I used to make a living. There was never a car that I fell in love with."

At 32 years of age, WJ decided it was time to go all in. He began preparing to race Pro Stock full time.

After logging five NHRA Pro Stock events in 1975, he competed in all eight races in 1976 and reached the final round three times. His first final was at Gainesville Raceway's NHRA Gatornationals.

"We had absolutely no backing, and we were racing out of our own pocket," said WJ in a 2003 interview for

Kurt and family friend Russell George are working on the engine at the edge of the family's box truck. Arlene took this photo at Union Grove's Great Lakes Dragaway in Wisconsin in 1974.

GM Performance. "Considering that we were competing against people like [Bob] Glidden and [Bill 'Grumpy'] Jenkins—established teams with substantial factory support—we were pretty happy to reach the final that early on. I took it as an omen that I could make it in this sport."

Finishing the season No. 2 in the Pro Stock points left WJ with a very clear picture of what the future could hold. He knew there was no time for self-congratulatory celebrations on a job well done. It was right back to work.

Winning Grand Am No. 9 in Tulsa as a family in 1974.

CHAPTER 4

FROM MATCH RACING TO A MAJOR SPONSOR

Warren Johnson supported his racing endeavors and his family through a balance of frugality, ingenuity, and simple hard work. For a gentleman who enjoyed racing and understood the formula for making money while doing it, opportunities were plentiful in the early years.

"I never considered it particularly difficult," admitted WJ. "Heck, if you can come out of northern Minnesota, you can survive racing. We went match racing, pro racing, all the UDRA stuff. Then, whatever it paid, you put it in the bank and were that much further away from poverty. I looked at match racing as an avocation, not a vocation. This was my hunting, fishing, gardening, and bowling all wrapped up in something with four tires on it."

Between the UDRA circuit in the Midwest, in which Johnson competed in 20 events and was named the Rookie of the Year in 1972, and the plentiful amount of racetracks scattered around the local area, WJ and his brood participated in a tremendous amount of match racing. He brought home a tidy sum each week. Although they didn't spend much time at home, and WJ was never left with any spare time, as he worked tirelessly to make what he had better.

The circuit evolved along with the popularity of Pro Stock. In 1972 and 1973, it was on full blast with events scheduled throughout the week by racetracks with highly effective promoters who repeatedly packed the house with folks who fiercely appreciated Pro Stock.

Warren Johnson heating up the tires of his 1970 Camaro with a little help from his friends at Minnesota Dragways in 1972. (Photo Courtesy John Foster Jr.)

WJ's 1970 Camaro is lost in a cloud of smoke as he concludes a burnout in front of a large crowd at a match race at Minnesota Dragways. (Photo Courtesy John Foster Jr.)

Mopar campaigner John Hagen, a fellow Minnesotan, was WJ's first rival—at least according to the announcer hyping up the stands at Minnesota Dragways in the early 1970s. (Photo Courtesy John Foster Jr.)

From the beginning, WJ seemed to grasp the full spectrum of positive and negative attributes in the sport of drag racing. "It's a law of diminishing returns. The faster you go, the harder it is to keep going faster," he said.

"They got 19,000 people in Minnesota Dragways one Sunday, and we raced John Hagen in his factory-backed Mopar," said WJ. "When those two cars were on the starting line, you could hear a pin drop."

John Foster Jr. was just a teenager when WJ was a regular at Minnesota Dragways. He recalls getting a read on the future legend relatively quickly as someone who didn't mince words when something was on his mind.

"He was a very spirited competitor," Foster said. "As best I remember, he spoke his piece, and you always knew where he stood. He was very professional, even then, and he wanted everyone else to be very professional too. He was a good racer and didn't appreciate people who didn't take it as seriously as he did."

WJ enjoyed competing at the facility, whether it was for a match race or a UDRA event. Minnesota Dragways was unique in that it had oversized safety zones, including a 3/4-mile shutdown that extended the length of the surface to an entire mile from the starting line to the end of the track. The track was wide with no guardrails or cement retaining walls, and it was one of the first to put on a four-wide show. The facility did this out of necessity, because with 600 or 700 cars entered, racing four across was the only way to expedite the process enough to get everyone through eliminations. The stands sat well back from the racetrack, but they would be filled for races that WJ ran, and cars would be parked well into the surrounding woods.

The racetrack was managed by Foster's parents, John Sr. and Marjorie Foster, and he worked his way into being something of an official track photographer. He drafted a catalog of images from the likes of WJ, John Hagen, Bill "Grumpy" Jenkins, the Sox & Martin team, Dave Strickler, Gapp & Roush, and many others who raced at the family's drag strip.

This photo was captured two years after WJ won his first trophy at Minnesota Dragways. WJ said that his first victory there was "the first of not enough. Nobody ever wins more than they lose." (Photo Courtesy Steve Reyes)

The Pro Stock Meet Recap

*This is an excerpt from the *"Drag News" from Minnesota Dragways* mailer Issue 11, July 11, 1971.

It was out of this world—14 cars—super runs—and action! WOW!!! All cars ran at 2 p.m. The best 8 ETs came back and ran for the money. Three of the pro cars were local—John Hagen of St. Paul, Rod Anderson of Duluth, and Warren Johnson of Minneapolis. Of these, only Warren Johnson of Competition Engine Builders made it and qualified, and from then on, the car to beat was WARREN JOHNSON! He looked and drove super! You should of seen the three 3-foot wheelstands in each gear and still turned a 10.15 ET and beat his competition, Bob Harvey. Right there the stage was set! Warren in the semifinals against

the best UDRA pros here. Man, the burnouts if you haven't seen how the Pro Stocks do it, you're just going to have to wait till the next meet! But they sure are something else. The tree goes green and they are off running—at the tree Warren Johnson is ahead, but wait—he is going up and I mean up! Never in the 11 years of drag racing here has there ever been a wheelstand like this one. He is on the rear bumper past the tower now. Wild, and down with a big crash, on all 4 wheels and losing the race to the eventual winner—Shelby Jester!

Where can you see the picture? The mighty Minneapolis Star had its Star photo man, Art Haber, on the scene all day for photos—and he got all the action! It was in the Wednesday evening Mpls. Star. If you didn't get it—find someone who did! Art works with Bob Schranck, who sure knows who to send out for top photos! Oh, incidentally, Warren Johnson now holds the highest wheelie out at Minnesota! And those beautiful Pro Stocks run again in open competition here August 22. Make it man—it's there!!!

The Competition Engine Service Inc. branding on the door of his 1970 Camaro was WJ's most prominent advertising of the business that he ran out of his four-stall garage in Fridley, Minnesota. This photo was taken in the summer of 1971 at Minnesota Dragways. (Photo Courtesy John Foster Jr.)

The match races between WJ and John Hagen, though, were among the most raucous. The fans in the stands backed their preferred brand: Johnson in the Chevrolet and Hagen in the Mopar. The announcer would rile the crowd, eliciting cheers from the Chevy loyalists that would be answered just as enthusiastically by the throngs of Mopar fans.

"It was a fun rivalry," said Foster. "There were never any staging issues or any of that kind of stuff that goes on today—they just respected each other as professional racers. It was good, clean racing, and everybody loved it."

WJ was careful with his winnings from Minnesota Dragways and every event he attended. He padded his financial stability with a healthy dose of resourcefulness. He only purchased the parts that he needed and fabricated anything and everything that he could. The Johnson family didn't take vacations or spend lavishly on household items. They recognized that their fiscal well-being was in their own hands; sponsorships weren't

"It's an unusual situation in my case because I never chased a sponsor," said WJ, shown here in 1972. "Every sponsor I had, came to me first. It was probably more of a case of them analyzing that I was going to be successful with or without them—so jumping on the bandwagon was only going to help both of us. I'm not bragging about it; that's the way it was." (Photo Courtesy John Foster)

Wheels Way Up

Warren Johnson has always raced to win, but he also relished the opportunity to put into practice the research, development, and ideas he had away from the track.

WJ viewed the Pro Stock meet at Minnesota Dragways in July 1971 as an opportunity to really dig into a few ideas he had been wanting to test—in particular, the usefulness of wheelie bars. The stunning results, captured by *Minneapolis Star* photographer Arthur Hager, definitively answered WJ's query while putting on a spectacular show for everyone in attendance.

"We thought if the wheelie bars were employed inefficiently, they probably hurt performance," said WJ. "We were playing with different styles: some axle-mounted, some chassis-mounted. As we went along, we figured that the other option was no wheelie bars at all."

So, the Professor removed the accessories in question and headed up to the lanes for the semifinals of an exhibition race that had kicked off with 16 Pro Stockers on the property. He was the fastest on the block that day, but his drive to win didn't do anything to squelch his deep drive to learn.

As he launched, the wheels came up incredibly fast, and the rear bumper made contact with the ground, tires spinning through the entire ordeal. Despite a windshield full of sky, WJ had the knowledge and wherewithal to shift gears to keep the horsepower high and hopefully lessen the impact when the front tires finally came back down to earth. The jolt was still enough to flatten the headers and the oil pan, bend the frame, and crack some of the fiberglass along the front of the Camaro's body.

"I was just trying to figure out how I was going to land the thing with a minimal amount of damage," said WJ. "It really wasn't too bad. It came down pretty straight, so it was a matter of coasting to the end of the track and bringing it back. Wheelie bars are required now, so the only option is to make them efficient. We eliminated one of the three options that day."

After the event, WJ diagnosed that he had about 54 percent of the weight on the rear tires, and it should have been approximately 52 percent.

Then 27 years of age, WJ went on to tell journalist Bob Schranck of the *Minneapolis Star,* "I don't particularly like driving, just the idea of getting it to work well. But I haven't found a driver I really trust."

The front end of WJ's Chevy required some attention following the massive wheelie at Minnesota Dragways in July 1971. According to WJ, though, it didn't take long before it was just fine and ready to race once more.

The wheelstand heard round the world—or at least by anyone who received the Minneapolis Star, *now known as the* Star Tribune. *(Photo Courtesy the* Star Tribune*)*

WJ got a big glimpse of sky after removing the wheelie bars during a series of functionality tests. The goal was to determine the most efficient way to run them—or if they were really needed. The test quickly confirmed that they were, in fact, a necessary feature. This image captures some of the wreckage after the car came down from the massive wheelstand at Minnesota Dragways in 1971.

common, and large sponsors were unheard of at that time.

"You'd have a few guys [who] gave a little bit of money here or there, but it didn't really amount to anything other than helping to pay the bills," WJ recalled. "But I just said, 'This is what I'm going to do, and dammit, I'm going to figure out a way.'"

Mid-1970s March

When WJ committed to full-time racing in 1976 without a backup plan, he began filling in races wherever he could, match racing, running the AHRA circuit, and entering all eight of the NHRA events. Midway through 1975, driving the 1974 Camaro that came to be known as *The Incredible Hulk*, WJ had already begun to garner attention in respected circles.

His success and efforts gave fresh life to the Chevrolet Camaro in Pro Stock, and a large part of the strides that he made early on was his eagerness to ask questions, listen, and learn. He continued to develop relationships with entities that catered their products to high performance, such as Weiand, Lenco, Hooker, Crane, and Amalie, and assisted with testing and development. Through those collaborations, his knowledge of the capabilities of the big-block Chevrolet compounded rapidly.

WJ had a background in product development that reached back into the 1960s, when he worked on the first successful tunnel ram manifold for a 427 of the time. His work with the rat engine design provided credibility that would open doors down the road and serve well in helping to cement his position as "the Professor."

The rumblings in the early 1970s on the AHRA circuit were that WJ had the fastest big-block Camaro in the country. In 1974, he had a big-block Vega built for match racing and continued to steadily build his case, as he would throughout his career, in almost any car he drove.

WJ claimed top speed on the circuit at six races in 1974, running just one engine the entire season and

WJ had been looking for a car that was smaller than the Camaro, and he landed on the Vega. "At that point in time, I was looking crudely at aerodynamics," he explained. (Photo Courtesy Auto Imagery)

WJ made the commitment to race full time in 1975 with this Camaro. He set national records with this trusty Chevrolet four times the following season, laying the groundwork for a career marked by speed and power. The first national record he claimed was in May 1976 at Denver's Bandimere Speedway, where he clocked a 156.66-mph pass to nudge past rival Bob Glidden's previous record of 156.52. WJ improved the record with a 157.78 in Marion, South Dakota, the following month, then reset it again in July with a 158.45 at Englishtown. A 158.73 at Montreal capped off his summer of speed. (Photo Courtesy Auto Imagery)

"The Vega was a manual 4-speed," said WJ. "I put 300 runs on it and never missed a shift running 8.6s at 160 mph. That car was way ahead of its time." (Photo Courtesy Auto Imagery)

The Camaro that WJ built for the 1975 season proved to be a sturdy companion. He drove the Chevy for four years and put thousands of runs on it, won national events in multiple sanctioning bodies, and scored the IHRA championship. Although, it would come to look a little less shiny over the years, eventually earning the nickname the Incredible Hulk. (Photo Courtesy Auto Imagery)

recording a best time of 8.73 at 159 mph. He made an abundance of runs that year, and the following season, performance picked up even more. In Tulsa, WJ was No. 3 behind the more experienced racers Bill Jenkins and Larry Huff.

The 1976 Bullet

WJ's 1974 Camaro was powered by a 427 Chevrolet with a special crankshaft that reduced displacement to 397 ci. WJ would leave the starting line at approximately 8,000 rpm and use 9,600-rpm shift points.

At the 1976 AHRA Springnationals, he was in his Camaro and raced to low ET, just missing top speed of the meet on an 8.830 with a 153-mph pass that was 0.04 second off the world record. It was the fastest run ever for a fully legal big-block Chevy. He fell in the final to Ford pilot "Dyno" Don Nicholson.

Then at the next race, WJ knocked out the Gapp & Roush Ford in the first round before he was ousted by Bill Jenkins and his Vega in the final. The already-fast Camaro was picking up speed—and notoriety.

The 1976 AHRA race at Tulsa's

Okie Nationals stoked a rivalry between WJ and defending series champion Ken Dondero, who was piloting Jenkins's Chevy Monza. This was one of two cars owned by Jenkins that raced in NHRA competition as well; Larry Lombardo raced the other.

WJ challenged Dondero to a one-round grudge race on Saturday night and lost by a handful of inches. Then

The Camaro that WJ piloted in the 1977 NHRA season bore the number 2 on the window. That's Gordie Rivera in the other lane at the Winternationals in Pomona. (Photo Courtesy Steve Reyes)

One Wild Ride

Warren Johnson celebrated his 34th birthday on July 7, 1977. The following day, a Friday, he was making a pass in his 3-year-old Camaro at what was then known as Madison Township Raceway Park in Englishtown, New Jersey, when he was faced with a very large problem.

After crossing the finish line on the qualifying run, WJ's brakes failed and his parachute would not deploy. Realizing he was in big trouble and quickly sorting through the limited options, WJ observed a gang of cars at the top end that he needed to avoid. Although it had initially crossed his mind to try to spin out at the top end, there was no room to do so. So, he veered off the right side of the track, crested a small hill, then wheeled down the embankment and through two fences before spinning out on bordering Pension Road.

Uninjured, WJ emerged and scooped up the busted fiberglass pieces while he waited for a tow. Once back inside the facility, the unperturbed racer went straight to the scales so as not to forfeit the run. His 8.83, 157.34 put a smile on his face.

"We finally got the mile-an-hour back in it," he said.

The cars of the 1980s, like the Oldsmobile Starfire that WJ drove to his first national event win and multiple national records, were learning devices for the Professor. In the 1990s, his Olds Cutlass and Pontiac Firebirds would reign supreme. (Photo Courtesy Steve Reyes)

on Sunday, the two were paired in the final round with grandstands packed. Johnson left first and never looked back, crossing the finish line with an 8.80 at 155.17 mph to his opponent's 8.87 at 154.70 mph.

Dondero locked down the AHRA championship that season, but WJ made him work for it. WJ would claim an IHRA crown for himself in 1981 with Jerome Bradford.

WJ was contending for the NHRA championship in 1976 while also chasing AHRA trophies and match racing. The man who came to be known as "the Professor" finished second in the world in the NHRA. At the time, NHRA Pro Stock ran division races, known as the World Championship Series (WCS), as well as national events.

Racers could claim events within their division, but they could also travel to other divisions in an attempt to block their adversaries from going rounds. WJ was counting points early, and by midseason he was strategizing to make appearances in Jenkins's neck of the woods to try and gain a little leverage.

Heading into the NHRA Finals, WJ was facing a 596 points deficit and knew the championship would take everything he had and then some. It was possible, but WJ would have to win the race, pray that Jenkins's driver Lombardo bowed out early, and break his own national record. The location of the event (Ontario Motor Speedway) was not prone to ideal conditions for Pro Stock records. The track had good "bite," but the air wasn't generally quite that favorable.

There was no record set, and Lombardo defeated WJ via a holeshot en route to the final round. When it was all said and done, WJ had put together a remarkable inaugural full-time season. It was not lost on a single soul that he was there to win, and a second-place finish for the year was disappointing, but it was also evidence of what the future would hold.

Oldsmobile Stakes Claim in Pro Stock

In 1979, the Oldsmobile representative involved in its motorsports program, Dale Smith, approached WJ at the *Popular Hot Rodding* meet in Martin, Michigan. Smith asked if WJ would be interested in running an Oldsmobile, and WJ replied, "Tell me what you've got and what kind of program you're trying to put together, and we'll talk."

The conversation at the facility now known as US 131 Motorsports Park was the beginning of one of the

The Professor's Way: Lesson 10

"I don't really believe in destiny," Warren Johnson said. "God designed us all with equal intelligence and opportunity. He also gave us two ears and one mouth, which means you should be listening twice as much as you're talking—and sometimes, that's how you find opportunity. My attitude has always been, do whatever it takes using whatever you have, and if you're only going to do something halfway, there's no sense in doing it at all. How much desire you have and how you cultivate your opportunities determine what the end result will be. How much sacrifice are you willing to endure to achieve your goals?"

longest and most notable partnerships in the history of drag racing. The first few years of WJ's involvement with Olds were with a small-block he ran in the Starfire. He later outfitted the car with a big-block for NHRA Pro Stock competition.

In the early days, there was no cash involved in WJ's partnership with Oldsmobile, only the provision of parts.

"But because I was successful with that small-block Oldsmobile—it was one of the very first cars to run 160 mph—they took note," stated WJ.

Shifting to the IHRA

NHRA Pro Stock experienced early growing pains, and one that WJ found particularly unfavorable was the introduction of weight breaks. According to the first edition of *The History of NHRA Pro Stock*, an NHRA-produced publication authored in part by Pro Stock historian John Jodauga, "Concerns about Chrysler's domination prompted NHRA officials to adopt a weight-break policy for 1972, which permitted straight inline-valve wedge engines to run at 6.75 pounds per cubic inch, staggered-valve engines to run at 7.00 pounds per cubic inch, and hemi cylinder head cars to weigh in at 7.26 pounds per cubic inch. Cars with wheelbases of less than 100 inches had a weight

minimum of 2,000 pounds, and those with more than 100 inches would run at 2,400 pounds."

This was only the beginning, though, as weight breaks were continuously adjusted throughout the decade. By 1980, almost every engine in Pro Stock had a separate weight break, and variation in wheelbase could change the equation. It was complicated, and it was expensive.

The constantly shifting rules were an honest attempt by the sanctioning body to level the playing field and keep one brand from having an unfair advantage, but the costly side effects were not acceptable to the ever-frugal WJ. In glaring contrast, IHRA rules mandated that the race car weigh in at no less than 2,350 pounds, but it didn't dictate engine size and kept a steady rule book.

"When the NHRA was factoring every engine combination, financially, I looked at that as a losing situation," said WJ. "You'd have to build a specific engine for [every] rule change, and I said, enough of that crap. So, I went to the IHRA in 1979 and was successful there, even with an engine that was 200 ci smaller than anything else out there. I still won because I took a more scientific approach.

"It was a lot simpler approach," he continued. "The IHRA saw all of the match racing going on, noticed the big crowds, and saw that everybody who match raced had an engine that was bigger than NHRA-legal outfitted with whatever it took to increase performance for a particular combination. The IHRA came up with some pretty set rules that weren't changing every week, and that appealed to me."

There were certainly other successful racers in the IHRA at the time, but WJ stood out in more ways than one. The car he won his first IHRA championship with

To Nitrous or Not to Nitrous?

"The only time I ever ran nitrous was when we would match race [Don] Nicholson. He would drain two 10-pound bottles in a run, so to keep up with him, you had to run nitrous," Warren Johnson said.

"It was eye-opening how powerful that stuff could be. It [picked up] two-tenths and 17 mph, and that was a small kit. That big, ugly Monte Carlo I drove for Jerome Bradford, you had to wait until you got it in second gear.

If it didn't shake the tires going into second gear, then you'd hit the button and hang on.

"But I really had no interest in the stuff. I don't like superchargers, turbochargers, or any boosted application. Obviously, if someone knew how to build an engine in the first place, they wouldn't have to put a power-adder to it. If all these people had an efficient engine to start with, they'd be badass sons of bitches."

was his 1974 Camaro nicknamed *the Incredible Hulk*. Though brutally fast, the car would not exactly have been labeled aesthetically pleasing.

A well-used piece, WJ estimated that the Chevrolet he piloted then had 3,500 to 4,000 runs on it during its championship season. The exterior was quite a sight with lightweight fiberglass installed everywhere it could possibly be used and a distinct, eye-catching paint scheme of Brandywine and primer.

"Taking the least-costly path to achieve results gave me an advantage, in some cases," observed WJ. "But it wasn't always pretty."

Another advantage WJ believed he had was how the racetracks were prepared in the series. His competitors were attempting to apply more power than the typical surface could hold, and after so many years of match racing, WJ knew how to get the most out of even the most questionable racetrack.

Georgia Calling

There is no disputing that Minnesota winters are cold, and they are long. WJ and his brood were more than open to laying down roots in a more welcoming climate, so when Atlanta-area businessman Jerome Bradford approached WJ about driving his Camaro in the IHRA's Mountain Motor Pro Stock class, it was a no-brainer.

The NHRA had "legislated the big-blocks right out of Pro Stock competition," according to WJ, who embraced IHRA's unrestricted cubic inch displacement. He won the 1979 IHRA Pro Stock championship with his 1974 Camaro and approximately 470 ci compared to the nearly 600-ci monstrosities of the majority of his competitors. That caught Bradford's eye, and the two formed a partnership for the 1980 season. They won the IHRA championship together with WJ behind the wheel of another Camaro owned by Bradford.

"If I was going to race, Minnesota was not the place we needed to be," said WJ, who also drove Bradford's Monte Carlo following their championship run together. "It was 40 miles from where God left his shoes. It was so far out of the loop, and those road expenses really cut into your profit. When you're located at a central point, you can feasibly test more. Minnesota race season is about three and

WJ ventured south to drive for the Atlanta-area businessman Jerome Bradford. WJ first wheeled his own Camaro, then Bradford's, then this Monte Carlo in IHRA competition. (Photo Courtesy Jim Kampmann)

a half months, and that's it. You can't put snow tires on a race car."

WJ quickly became a fan of the area and had a house built in Georgia. Kurt was still in high school, so the family kept their Minnesota residence for the time being, traveling south to race and work as necessary.

WJ's engine business in Fridley, Minnesota, was thriving, but as was the case with anything he started in his life, he was able to shift gears completely and focus on the next opportunity with little to no attachment to the past. Competition Engine Service Inc. was left behind without much, if any, heartache.

"I was doing quite a bit of round-track work and whatnot, but there were plenty of other engine shops in the Minneapolis/St. Paul area," said a very matter-of-fact WJ. "They could absorb whatever workload I left behind, so I guess it worked out for everybody.

"Down South, everything was geared toward the IHRA program, so I didn't really build anything outside of that when I moved down there. It was just Bradford, and that obviously worked."

The morning after Kurt graduated, he and his dad were on a plane to Georgia. They needed to get to Bradford's shop and prepare for the next IHRA event, which was to take place in Norwalk, Ohio.

The Johnson family marked that day as the day Kurt left home.

"It was time to go," Kurt said and smiled. "I moved in with Bradford. He was single at the time and running the construction company. I worked at the race car shop, Dad flew in every now and again, we went racing, and it was all good."

Kurt moved out of Bradford's place six months after arriving and got his own apartment. Before too long, his girl from Minnesota, Kathy, joined him. They were married in 1985.

Warren and Arlene sold the house up north and moved everything to Georgia, where they eventually built a 26,000-square-foot shop in Sugar Hill. The shop

eventually housed 97 national event wins and 6 NHRA championships for WJ and 40 hard-fought Pro Stock trophies for KJ along with regular top-10 finishes.

The move was a gigantic testament to the family's unrelenting commitment to racing as a business.

"To be successful in racing, you really had to live it every day," said WJ. "It's a lifestyle, there are no two ways about it, especially the way I chose to do it. I had to make a profit. Period. End of story. I had to figure out how to run a business, because I'd never been to business school, and how to make it profitable and self-sustaining. But that's always made it interesting. I look at every day as a new opportunity to do something different and, hopefully, better."

Johnson's second championship was wrapped up at Atmore Dragway's IHRA World Title Series event behind the wheel of Bradford's Camaro. The season started off on a bit of a dire note, as Johnson missed the opener at South Carolina's Darlington Dragway. Ronnie Sox piloted his Sox & Martin Omni to victory there, then again in Rockingham at the Pro-Am Nationals.

WJ missed a milestone by missing Rockingham, where Rickie Smith blasted into the IHRA Holley 7-Second Club with a 7.99-second pass at 172.41 in his *Oak Ridge Boys* Mustang.

WJ returned to the circuit for the IHRA Spring Nationals and found that Glidden had brought his Fairmont to the playground. Smith sent his fellow Ford campaigner packing in round two, though, and WJ went on to claim the event title in a repeat of his efforts there the year prior. His post-race meeting with the press ignited a telephone game within the Mountain Motor Pro Stock ranks, and the original message of "this will be WJ's last race of the year" passed along in rapid fashion.

The class was more than pleased with the idea of having the defending series champion out of the picture, but team owner Bradford didn't take kindly to the suggestion of a short season. He used whatever means he could to convince WJ to continue.

The championship came down to WJ and Smith in the final hours. Smith had gotten the nod over a red-lighting Don Nicholson at Thunder Valley Dragway in Bristol. It was his first victory of the season, and it threw fuel on the fire that raged between him and WJ. Their fight went on for the next two events.

WJ clocked an eighth-mile record of 5.09, 139 in the Atmore Dragway final to turn away a dejected Smith and adjust the championship crown that would rest upon

Seen here in November 1982, Kurt traveled with his father to all of the IHRA races and actually took up residence in Jerome Bradford's home for a short while until getting settled in a place of his own. KJ was the lead crewmember even before graduating from high school, and he logged many hours in Bradford's shop, preparing the race car and fine-tuning things that had gotten out of whack at any given event.

KJ having a rest in the race trailer one weekend brought about some razzing. Someone crafted a sign for him that read, "Too much fun in the sun."

After WJ and Arlene moved to Georgia permanently, they began construction on Warren Johnson Enterprises, the expansive race shop that would truly become home for them.

The structure is going up for the 26,000-square-foot race shop.

Here is the view of the back of the brand-new Warren Johnson Enterprises building.

This is the front of the newly completed structure that WJ had built to house his racing operation.

Inside of the Warren Johnson Enterprises shop, there is a cutout that leads to the upstairs warehouse. With a fork-lift, a Pro Stock car could be raised and stored there.

One of WJ's Pro Stockers en route to its resting place in the warehouse upstairs at the WJE shop.

WJ's Olds Cutlass is at rest in its new home inside the Warren Johnson Enterprises race shop.

The critical addition to any racing operation, but particularly to WJ's, was the appropriate machinery to craft everything he needed for his program. Proper machinery allowed for greater, more efficient research and development—WJ's specialty. Here is the machinery being installed in the new building.

Tales from the Strip

After winning his second IHRA championship, Jerome Bradford put WJ in the driver's seat of his new car: a 1981 Monte Carlo. In comparison to the sleek Camaro Pro Stockers that WJ had wheeled in the past (both his own and Bradford's), the Monte Carlo was boxy and bulky with a broad front end that wasn't capable of slicing through the air with efficiency.

"It had zero downforce in the rear, and it didn't matter how much spoiler you put on it," said WJ, who outfitted the Monte Carlo with a 500-ci bullet capable of turning 8,500 rpm. "But Bradford wanted a car that was different than everybody else, and that was about as different as you could get. If you could survive that car for a season, you could drive just about anything."

One weekend at Brainerd International Raceway, WJ and fellow Minnesotan John Hagen were set to race one another in the second round. They agreed beforehand that they would only do one burnout (two were customary in that setting at that time), but no one had told the track photographer. He positioned himself ahead of the two Pro Stockers right up by the starting lights to get the shot. The photographer had planned to quickly skirt away while the two did their second burnouts, but instead they began to stage after a single go at warming the tires. He was stuck.

Once staged, WJ brought the RPM up, as normal, but the starting lights didn't come on, and his engine began to feel the strain. The starter had refused to trigger the lights with the photographer there, and the result was a broken stud on an intake rocker arm that rendered one

Jerome Bradford's Monte Carlo is shown as piloted by WJ in 1981. Bradford, who dealt in heavy grading and site-preparation for retail establishments, had been involved in drag racing for some time. He wanted to increase his involvement (but as an owner rather than a driver) and found a good partner in Warren Johnson. (Photo Courtesy Jim Kampmann)

cylinder useless. WJ still won the round over Hagen with an 8.20-second pass, but the two quickest ETs of the semifinals were to be paired for the final, and WJ's did not make the cut.

Harold Denton beat Ronnie Sox in the final. Afterward, WJ returned to the starting line with his Monte Carlo. He had a point to prove, and he did so by laying down a 7.87 at 176.81 mph to record the car's best time, match the state record that he already held, and set the BIR Pro Stock record for speed.

his head for the second consecutive season.

In all, WJ won 13 IHRA Ironman trophies. He also claimed triumph in the American Hot Rod Association (AHRA), making the first 7-second Pro Stock pass (7.93 seconds) en route to his 1981 victory at the AHRA Gateway Nationals in St. Louis.

"Financially, racing with Bradford was great for me, and he got what he wanted: recognition as a car owner," WJ said. "He gave us free rein to do whatever we wanted, as far as running the car. He never interfered at all. Jerome Bradford was one of the best car owners any-

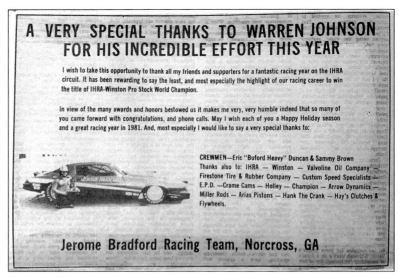

A VERY SPECIAL THANKS TO WARREN JOHNSON FOR HIS INCREDIBLE EFFORT THIS YEAR

I wish to take this opportunity to thank all my friends and supporters for a fantastic racing year on the IHRA circuit. It has been rewarding to say the least, and most especially the highlight of our racing career to win the title of IHRA-Winston Pro Stock World Champion.

In view of the many awards and honors bestowed us it makes me very, very humble indeed that so many of you came forward with congratulations, and phone calls. May I wish each of you a Happy Holiday season and a great racing year in 1981. And, most especially I would like to say a very special thanks to:

CREWMEN—Eric "Buford Heavy" Duncan & Sammy Brown
Thanks also to: IHRA — Winston — Valvoline Oil Company — Firestone Tire & Rubber Company — Custom Speed Specialists — E.P.D. —Crame Cams — Holley — Champion — Arrow Dynamics — Miller Rods — Arias Pistons — Hank The Crank — Hay's Clutches & Flywheels.

Jerome Bradford Racing Team, Norcross, GA

After winning the IHRA championship together in 1980, team owner Jerome Bradford took out this grateful advertisement in Drag Review. The clipping is pasted in one of the many scrapbooks kept by Arlene Johnson. "I enjoyed racing. It was hectic, but it was always interesting. It kept you going," she said.

This Drag Review *clipping out of Arlene's 1979 scrapbook explains that WJ "took the Winston-IHRA series by storm" as he charged to his first championship. "The IHRA program prepared me for what it takes to be competitive at the national level," said WJ, years later. "You have to understand how to win; winning doesn't happen by accident. I learned how to race there."*

This photo was taken after WJ won his first IHRA championship on Sunday, September 30, 1979, at Atlanta.

Year	Event	Location
1979	Northern Nationals	Milan, Michigan
1979	Spring Nationals	Bristol, Tennessee
1979	Winston Nationals	Atlanta, Georgia
1980	Dixie Nationals	Atlanta, Georgia
1980	Spring Nationals	Bristol, Tennessee
1981	Northern Nationals	Milan, Michigan
1981	Spring Nationals	Bristol, Tennessee
1982	U.S. Open Nationals	Rockingham, North Carolina
1982	Pro-Am Nationals	Rockingham, North Carolina
1988	Chief Nationals	Dallas, Texas
1988	Spring Nationals	Bristol, Tennessee
1988	Fall Nationals	Bristol, Tennessee
1989	Spring Nationals	Bristol, Tennessee

body could have, especially at the time when I was basically learning the ropes of what it takes to be successful in racing."

Behind the scenes, WJ's opportunities were expanding. He was on the cusp of making a move that would become the launching pad for his place in Pro Stock history.

"Oldsmobile approached me about doing a program," said WJ. "So, I was working on that at the same time that I was racing IHRA. I had a lot more on my plate than I probably needed, but I'd say it worked out."

WJ and Frank Iaconio square off at a match race in Martin, Michigan, in 1983. Iaconio was a fearsome competitor and fellow Pro Stock engine builder. From 1980 to 1984, WJ, Iaconio, Bob Glidden, and Lee Shepherd monopolized the Pro Stock winner's circle. "We were all just trying to win races," said WJ. "Looking back, I don't think it was particularly good for the category or for the competition. When a category is monopolized by just a few racers, it loses some of its appeal for both the spectators and the competitors." (Photo Courtesy Steve Reyes)

CHAPTER 5

CROSSING THE THRESHOLD OF SUCCESS

Pro Stock was born in the National Hot Rod Association (NHRA) in 1970 from the Super Stock and Factory Experimental classes. The establishment of the new category didn't just pave the way, it kicked in the door for massive strides in technological advancement. Just a handful of years into the rise of the class, complete tube-chassis frames came into play, three- and four-link rear ends replaced stock suspension and leaf springs, and Lenco planetary gear clutchless 4-speed transmissions were employed.

Concentrated, precise attention to cylinder heads and porting became mandatory if there was to be measurable success, and Warren Johnson, a *precisioneer* by nature, was right at home. After getting his first taste of the NHRA scene at the 1971 U.S. Nationals in Indianapolis, WJ focused his energy on the match racing circuit. In 1975, he dipped into NHRA competition again, this time competing in five events and finishing just outside of the top 10 for the year.

As his active education in racing continued, upward momentum increased. At that time, Pro Stock was also contested at points meets, and in 1976 WJ won each of the five Division 5 races. By season's end, he held the class record with a 158.73-mph pass. In 1976, he finished No. 2 in the Pro Stock standings with eight NHRA races on record for the year.

WJ's 1974 Camaro got a lot of mileage in both NHRA and IHRA competition. Here it is in 1978 at the Summernationals in Englishtown. WJ took his Chevrolet Camaro to the IHRA and won the championship there in 1979. Atlanta contractor Jerome Bradford took notice, and they partnered together the next season for a championship run. (Photo Courtesy Keith Cyr/Race Dog Photography)

KJ plays in the staging lanes while his father converses with a fellow racer.

KJ had numerous racetrack friends growing up. This is Chris Lang using a floor jack at Donnybrooke in July 1971. In the background is Ricky Lappi, Kathy Lang (on the truck), and KJ.

NHRA Pro Stock Steadies

For the 1982 season, the NHRA laid out new rules for Pro Stock: 500-ci engines would run heads-up. The straightforward approach stabilized the class and drew participants into a new and hardy era of Pro Stock.

Clearly, larger engines came with more performance potential. So, the rules were also adjusted to allow for a rear spoiler with a height of 6 inches, an increased maximum hood-scoop height of 10 inches, and relocation of the driver's seat to farther back in the cockpit.

"The NHRA saw the success the IHRA was having with what they called 'Mountain Motor Pro Stock' cars. They saw the crowd response, and they saw the disenchantment of their own racers. They had to do something," said WJ. "I really didn't have a clue what engine displacement they were going to have, but it appeared they were going to stabilize the rules, and that, coupled with Olds wanting to get involved with its own engine [the Drag Racing Competition Engine, or DRCE], solidified the whole program for me."

WJ entered the 1982 season of NHRA Pro Stock with his self-sponsored Oldsmobile Starfire powered by a big-block Chevy. He quickly proved that he was going to

This Oldsmobile Starfire that WJ affectionately referred to as Butterbean was campaigned in both the IHRA and then in NHRA in 1982. Although WJ viewed the NHRA's 1982 rule change to 500-ci engines and heads-up racing for Pro Stock as a welcome shift, he wasn't overly enthusiastic about it. "I tend to not get excited about anything. Mistakes are made when you're excited," he stated. Then, he added with a grin, "Marriage is proof of that." (Photo Courtesy Steve Reyes)

Longstanding friendships were formed repeatedly through the years as the Johnson family traveled the various circuits. Crewman John Caruso with Anne Lepone are shown in this photo from an NHRA event. Joe Sr. and Anne Lepone were good friends of the Johnsons and would visit whenever they could. Joe Sr. was particularly fond of Arlene and always called her "Doll Baby."

Joe Lepone Sr. got hold of a WJ T-shirt and was determined to squeeze into it. It was a tight fit, but Joe made it work.

The NHRA's 1982 Pro Stock Scorecard			
Event	**Location**	**Winner**	**Runner-up**
Winternationals	Pomona, California	Frank Iaconio	Lee Shepherd
Gatornationals	Gainesville, Florida	Lee Shepherd	Frank Iaconio
Southern Nationals	Atlanta, Georgia	Lee Shepherd	Bob Glidden
Cajun Nationals	Baton Rouge, Louisiana	Lee Shepherd	Frank Iaconio
Springnationals	Columbus, Ohio	Bob Glidden	Lee Shepherd
Grandnationals	Montreal, Quebec, Canada	Lee Shepherd	Warren Johnson
Summernationals	Englishtown, New Jersey	Warren Johnson	Lee Shepherd
Mile-High Nationals	Denver, Colorado	Lee Shepherd	Bob Glidden
Northstar Nationals	Brainerd, Minnesota	Lee Shepherd	Frank Iaconio
U.S. Nationals	Indianapolis, Indiana	Frank Iaconio	Bob Glidden
Golden Gate Nationals	Fremont, California	Warren Johnson	Lee Shepherd
World Finals	Orange County, California	Warren Johnson	Lee Shepherd

The Professor's Way: Lesson 11

"People always talk about feeling pressure in a situation or being intimidated by the task at hand," Warren Johnson said. "I never felt pressure, and I never understood that way of looking at things. I knew what I had to do, and when you know what you have to do, how can you say there's any pressure? Pressure is generally self-induced. To be fully qualified for a particular job, you can't allow yourself to feel pressure."

be a player on the new-and-improved field. By the time the 13-race season hit the halfway point, WJ had become more than a player—he was a threat.

WJ reached his first final of the year at the 1982 Grandnationals in Montreal with his short-wheelbase Oldsmobile Starfire, but Lee Shepherd won the match. At the very next race, though, Englishtown's Summernationals, it was WJ who hoisted the trophy as the 18th NHRA Pro Stock winner in the history of the class.

"I remember beating Lee Shepherd, but it didn't really stick out to me that we were achieving anything," said WJ, who turned the tables with an upset in a neck-and-neck race. Times were 7.903 to 7.914. "It was my first NHRA win, but I had won in IHRA, and a win is a win. To me, there's no such thing as a bad win or a good loss."

The win was not particularly impactful to WJ, at least not in hindsight, but it was a pivotal moment for the Oldsmobile brand, as it was its first NHRA Pro Stock win. Part of what led to the victory that day might surprise some, and for WJ, the details simply enhanced the entertainment value of the memory.

"It was kind of a funny story," recalled WJ as his smile widened. "I'd match raced Englishtown on Wednesday nights half a dozen times during the year, so I knew what the track was going to be like. I went and got the oldest pair of Firestone tires I could find because they were bigger in diameter than the Goodyears everyone was using. Goodyear had won like 200 consecutive Pro Stock races, and here comes this stumblebum to break their streak with a pair of Firestones that were easily 3 or 4 years old. They were irritated."

A 180-mph Pin in the Map

In 1982, there was no doubt that a performance barrier would be broken as drivers inched closer and closer to the 180-mph mark.

The Olds Starfire was a good car for WJ, who won his first national event with it and also broke the 180-mph barrier with a 181.08 at Fremont's Golden Gate Nationals in 1982. WJ told Oldsmobile representative Dale Smith in 1978, "I'll race anything; I'm not particular." Smith started shipping parts, WJ started fooling with them in his Starfire, and the decades-long partnership was born. (Photo Courtesy Auto Imagery)

Entering the season, Minnesotan John Hagen held the record for speed at 165.13 mph, which he set at the World Finals at Orange Country International Raceway the previous October. Under the new rules, Lee Shepherd obliterated Hagen's record at the season-opening Pomona Winternationals, rocketing to a 174.75 that would only hold until the next race.

In Gainesville, Shepherd bettered the speed record with a 177.16. Then, in Montreal in July, he broke it again, as he clocked a blistering 178.57-mph pass. But then came September and the U.S. Nationals, and WJ had been picking up steam. The Oldsmobile Starfire was charging at Indy. WJ clocked top speed of the meet with a new national record of 179.28.

"After that, we made a last-minute decision to go to Fremont," recalled WJ. "I looked at the weather conditions and thought we should be able to go over 180, so we loaded up and away we went."

WJ was well aware of what it felt like to stand atop the pack, and he

"From an engine-guy standpoint, I suppose I'd value speed over elapsed time," said WJ, shown here with son, KJ. "Speed is usually indicative of power, but in my case, my car was more efficient. Did I really have more power? No one will ever know. I learned that lesson from Junior Johnson. I was doing some stuff for NASCAR at the time, and I asked him why his cars won more races than anyone. He was sitting there in bib overalls and a torn T-shirt, and he just looked at me. 'I put the wheels on right,' was all he said. That's a pretty big statement when you start dissecting it and looking for the inner, hidden meaning."

wasn't new to setting national records in NHRA competition. In fact, he reset the speed record four times in his 1976 Pro Stock campaign. However, then the cars were inching toward 160 mph. Shepherd would be the first to breach the milestone with a 160.71-mph pass at the 1978 Cajun Nationals in Baton Rouge.

A mere four years later, the factory hot rods were going 20 mph faster.

"My cars have always been noted to run speed, simply because I put the wheels on right," said WJ. "We didn't do anything special to achieve any of the milestones we reached; it was just a natural progression. Parts change, engine components change, so you keep working on things, massaging them all the time, hoping you pick up power. We generally found that we did."

The Johnson family arrived at the Golden Gate Nationals at Fremont Dragstrip (then known as Baylands) and set about its work. There wasn't anything terribly unusual that sticks out in WJ's mind about that day or the qualifying session in which he fired off a 7.70 at 181.08-mph shot that busted the barrier. It was more a case of everything falling into place.

"It was a different situation then because we really didn't have an engine dyno," explained WJ, who made

the record-setting pass in the first round of qualifying. "You looked at the time card at the end of the track, and then went to work on the spark plugs. That's how I tuned engines back then—I learned how to read spark plugs relatively well to know what I needed to do as far as the engine tune-up. I just kept picking at it, and it finally came around."

The barrier-breaking pass that WJ made was at the very top of a list of remarkable notes for the weekend at the Golden Gate Nationals. At the same event, Shepherd recorded the NHRA's first 7.60 pass with a 7.69 at 177 to take the pole. The No. 1 qualifier went on to clock a national record of 7.65, and WJ nearly edged him for the honor, answering with a 7.66.

Bob Glidden recorded a career best 7.68 to join them in the 7.60s, and every other Pro Stock racer on the property recorded career best times. Frank Iaconio in his new Don Ness Camaro (7.74), Don Coonce in Albert Clark's Camaro (7.78), Bob Ingles (7.79), Joe Lepone in Jenkins's Camaro (7.81), and Harry Scribner (7.84) all ran personal bests to establish the quickest eight-car Pro Stock field ever.

WJ won the event with a final-round triumph over Shepherd, who eventually snatched the speed record back—but not for almost a full year. The events of the

The Professor's Way: Lesson 12

"There are a lot of things that don't work the way you expect them to, and that's usually because you didn't include enough facts in your thought process," Warren Johnson said. "But that shouldn't create disappointment. It's all part of the learning experience. That's why I don't throw anything away. I store it upstairs [at the shop] so I can look back at it and say, 'Dumbass, what the hell were you thinking?'"

weekend were particularly notable after WJ revealed that the 181, made on the first pass of the weekend, had wounded his only engine. He told the press after the event that from then on, it was a case of minimizing damage while extracting the most power he possibly could.

In the final round, WJ was off the starting line ahead of Shepherd by a smidge in his Olds Starfire, and WJ clocked a 7.69 at 179.28 to his challenger's 7.74 at 179.20.

The road to 180 wasn't without its share of drama. Before making the milestone run at Fremont, NHRA Tech Director Cloy Fitzgerald had questions, as WJ was significantly faster than the rest of the field.

"He walked over to me and asked if the cylinder heads were legal," WJ chuckled. "He said, 'If they're not, you'll never race NHRA the rest of your life.' I looked at him and said, 'Those cylinder heads were built by your rule book. If you don't know how to interpret your own rule book, then you've got a problem.' They checked them over, and it took them about four hours to decide. There were four or so of them, and they all stood there looking at each other. Then one of them said, 'According to our rule book, these cylinder heads are absolutely 100-percent legal.' It was just that nobody had thought about how to build a cylinder head the way I did."

Although statistics, victories, and milestones are commonly accepted forms of quantifying achievement, WJ has never been much impressed by his own accomplishments. When he pushed the button to launch a full-time career in drag racing, he didn't lay out a timeline or goalposts that would determine when he had reached the summit.

"I just always looked at it from the standpoint, if I'm going to do this, I better be successful," he said. "Obviously, first and foremost I had to make money at it. To do that, I had to win races. It wasn't like one morning I woke up and said, 'Eureka! I'm here!' I just put my nose to the grindstone and got to work. This is my job. That's it. End of story."

WJ, ever a realist, didn't dream that his partnership with Oldsmobile would grow in the way that it did. He certainly never envisioned its stunning longevity.

"You just didn't know how long these programs would last," said WJ. "But I was very happy with my involvement with Oldsmobile because part of it was that I got to design whatever I wanted. The DRCE-1, -2, and -3 are all a result of that."

Oldsmobile saw an opportunity in the Pro Stock category, and the time was right to make a big splash as the 15th anniversary of the Hurst/Olds approached. Initially, another engineer was on the project of developing the world's first factory-block and cylinder-head combination for drag racing, but that changed as the project due date approached.

The brand intended to debut the Drag Race Competition Engine (DRCE) in 1983 in the commemorative Hurst/Olds Cutlass, but progress had stalled by the fall of 1982. Sources conflict as to how and why, but in any event, WJ ended up with the reins. Where the first engineer left off, WJ stepped in and brought the project to life. Due in large part to his efforts, Oldsmobile's DRCE was introduced in 1983 as intended.

WJ was setting records all along the path to 97 national event wins and 6 NHRA championships, including making the first hit that surpassed 180 mph. KJ, learning from the best, set a massive record of his own 12 years later when he was the first NHRA Pro Stock driver to break into the 6-second zone.

"After the first eight or nine months, [he] had a drawing of what he thought the intake port should look like, but that was as far as it had gone," said WJ, who landed the project with little time remaining before it was to debut in 1983. "I built the core boxes and had the first cylinder heads and blocks cast the way I wanted them in 10 days. It was such a rush job, we never even put that engine on the dyno."

The tiny window of time to put the brand-new engine program together was neither stressful nor prohibitive to Johnson.

"To me, it was nothing," he said. "It's what I do. You get the job done and shut up."

Although WJ wasn't flapping his gums about it, the engine spoke loud enough for everyone to hear. He debuted the striking black Hurst/Olds Cutlass with pleasing results.

"We went to the race and qualified No. 1 with the engine on its first pass ever," said WJ. He then smiled and said, "Glidden was fit to be tied."

Initiative and Innovation Ignite DRCE Project

Through the years, the DRCE gained respect as a powerplant that would withstand test after test, reach milestone after milestone, and become the cornerstone of performance for GM competitors in the field of drag racing.

As Arlene took a more active role in the race team, other wives were also finding their groove as important team members doing more than cooking and minding the children. Karen Holschlag is seen here with Arlene under the tower at an unidentified NHRA event.

"The DRCE was the beginning of innovation for this class," WJ said. "I'm not saying I was the right guy for the job, I just happened to be the one who went ahead and did it. I suppose somebody could have done a better job, but history is what it is. As they say, the stars aligned."

At the time of print, DRCE-2 and DRCE-3 engines

Warren Johnson Firsts	
First	Details
Drag race	Minnesota Dragways, 1963
Race car	1957 Chevrolet C/Modified Production
Win	Bracket race (Minnesota Dragways), 1963
NHRA race	1971 U.S. Nationals, Indianapolis
NHRA final round	1976 Gatornationals, Gainesville, Florida
NHRA victory	1982 Summernationals, Englishtown, New Jersey
Championship	1979 IHRA Pro Stock
NHRA Pro Stock championship	1992
NHRA Top Speed record	1976 Springnationals, Columbus, Ohio (156.25 mph)
NHRA No. 1 qualifier	1978 Springnationals, Columbus, Ohio (8.63 seconds)
180-mph Pro Stock run	181.08 mph (October 1, 1982, Fremont, California)
190-mph Pro Stock run	190.07 mph (August 29, 1986, Indianapolis, Indiana)
200-mph Pro Stock run	200.13 mph (April 25, 1997, Richmond, Virginia)
Father vs. Son final round in NHRA history	Warren Johnson defeated Kurt Johnson (April 25, 1993, Commerce, Georgia)
Father and son to finish 1st and 2nd in NHRA championship	1993 (Warren Johnson, No. 1, 17,008 points; Kurt Johnson No. 2, 13,502 points)
Data is based on notes from the GM Performance Parts Warren Johnson 2005 Media Guide.	

WJ in the striking Hurst/Olds, powered by the new Drag Race Competition Engine (DRCE), at Atlanta Dragway in 1983. The collaboration with Oldsmobile for its new DRCE was a project that WJ had worked hard and fast on to bring it to life for the new year. "The season was approaching, and somebody had to take the bull by the horns, so to speak," said WJ of DRCE development prior to the 1983 season. "I looked back at the lack of progress in what was basically a year, and I said, 'This isn't going to cut it.' So, I took it upon myself to do it." (Photo Courtesy Auto Imagery)

The Professor's Way: Lesson 13

"I make calculated errors," Warren Johnson said. "You have to understand (a) what you're trying to accomplish, (b) what you have to work with, and (c) how to put it together. You can't solve a problem unless you understand it, and first of all, you have to recognize that the problem exists. It's a lot like being addicted to drugs: you have to acknowledge that you have the problem before you can begin to work toward solving it."

The Hurst/Olds made appearances outside of the NHRA as well, as captured here in 1983 at US 131 Motorsports Park at Martin, Michigan. That's Reid Whisnant and his Dodge Omni in the near lane. (Photo Courtesy Steve Reyes)

The Hurts/Olds wads the rear tires on the launch. (Photo Courtesy Steve Reyes)

WJ leaves the starting line in the boxy but beautiful Hurst/Olds. (Photo Courtesy Steve Reyes)

Warren Johnson's iconic Hurst/Olds in 1984. (Photo Courtesy Steve Reyes)

"The DRCE was significantly better than anything out there because without making any test runs or even putting it on the dyno, we went out there at the first race and went to No. 1," said WJ, shown here racing Lee Shepherd in 1984 at the Northstar Nationals in Brainerd, Minnesota. "It's gotten a lot more sophisticated since then, but you have to remember that race cars damn near had wood-spoke wheels on them in those days. They were pretty crude." (Photo Courtesy Steve Reyes)

WJ's Hurst/Olds is shown in 1984 at Pomona. When asked about the other manufacturers and their engine development as it compared to GM's DRCE, WJ said, "Ford made a stab at it but had a totally misguided cylinder head on it. The block was pretty good. The Mopar Hemi was competitive, but if you look at it realistically, all the Ford and Mopar Pro Stock cars have DRCE engines in them now. They got rid of the corporate rule. I guess you could say that the proof is in the pudding." (Photo Courtesy Steve Reyes)

The Hurst/Olds had a different look in the 1984 season, but it still had the powerful DRCE under the hood. (Photo Courtesy Auto Imagery)

WJ crosses the finish line at the U.S. Nationals in 1984. (Photo Courtesy Steve Reyes)

have been at the heart of some of the most successful Pro Stock campaigns of all time. Every major GM Pro Stock team has had at least one version of the DRCE in its stable, and no other manufacturer has seen such lasting success.

"Oldsmobile wanted its own identity in Pro Stock, and that fit right into my wheelhouse," said WJ. "I enjoy designing things and doing something different. I really like trying to perfect things, and this gave me the opportunity to fix all the defects, as far as our drag racing pro-

gram was concerned."

In simple terms, WJ assessed the shortcomings of the big-block Chevrolet in relation to how it could perform in drag racing, and he attempted to fix them.

It took a few iterations to make significant improvements, but WJ wasn't intimidated by the magnitude of the work or rattled by the process of ironing out the wrinkles. Without time to get approval from a committee, he jumped right in and just kept going. He pulled up his chair to the draft table and created the pattern work for the prototype needed to cast the cylinder heads.

WJ hustled to produce the very first DRCE in time for the 1983 season. The sanctioning body, though, wasn't quite ready to sign off on the project.

"The NHRA wouldn't allow me to run the engine unless I supplied machined cylinder heads to everybody who wanted them, so that took about three months to produce," recalled WJ. "They probably presented it as a goal to keep a level playing field, but in reality, it

The DRCE-powered Firenza runs during a closed test session ahead of the 1987 campaign. The following season, WJ's engines would find their home in Oldsmobile's Cutlass model.

was strictly a knee-jerk reaction to a certain Ford racer screaming and hollering that somebody was going to have an advantage.

"The politics were unbelievable. When the NHRA approved what I was going to do, Glidden sat on the scales at Orange County and wouldn't let anybody go across because he was protesting. It was like a kid you'd taken candy away from."

Once he made it through all of the red tape, WJ was off and running with a plethora of power that his com-petitors could also access. He finished No. 4 in the nation that year, and then came back to finish No. 2 in five of the next eight seasons before earning his first NHRA champi-onship in 1992. This was after the DRCE received a major facelift in 1991 that centered around a better casting for the cylinder head.

"The original pattern work was done in such haste that we really didn't have time to finesse it, so in the early 1990s, the cylinder head was redone and com-pletely retooled," WJ said in GM press material.

Greg Anderson, Buzzy Woitas, and KJ go over one of the DRCE engines at a race in 1988. KJ and Anderson went on to race themselves, both with DRCE engines.

WJ began 1988 in the Olds Ciera but was in a Cutlass by Houston.

Although it was only around for a short while, WJ was in an Oldsmobile Ciera at the start of the 1988 season. Here it is under construction before the NHRA Winternationals.

Kurt and WJ discuss the upcoming run over the top of the race car.

Like Minds

When the Hurst/Olds was ready for its close-up, *Hot Rod* magazine put together a photo shoot with Miss Hurst Linda Vaughn and WJ's new ride. Vaughn already knew of WJ and had seen him race, and like anyone in drag racing, WJ was already well aware of the existence of Miss Vaughn. The collaboration of WJ and the Hurst/Olds brand spawned a lifelong friendship between Vaughn and the entire Johnson clan.

The photo shoot for the *Hot Rod* magazine cover took place in Miami on a very hot day, and Miss Hurst recalled that the red jumpsuit she had made out of a Bill Simpson Pro Stock parachute was not at all breathable. But the day was still enjoyable, and the cover, with Vaughn leaning on the hood of the Hurst/Olds in the striking-though-suffocating jumpsuit, is stunning.

"We had fun. Pro Stock was a big family; we looked out for each other," said Vaughn. "WJ and Grumpy Jenkins were my two biggest heroes. Neither one of them talked much, but when they did, you listened. I just love WJ, the Professor. He's done so much, and I really admire his accomplishments."

WJ explained that they connected immediately because Vaughn grew up in a rural community, just as he did.

"Both of us enjoyed what we were doing in life, though she was much more successful than I was," he said. "We were both of the same mindset though. I always had a new joke for her. We still get along great."

The lovely Linda Vaughn and the Hurst/Olds are ready for their close-up at a photo shoot for **Hot Rod** magazine in Florida.

Miss Hurst selected the fabric and had her jumpsuit made for the photo shoot.

The Johnsons made lifelong friends in racing, including Linda Vaughn, whom they met thanks to their partnership with Oldsmobile and the stunning Hurts/Olds in 1983 with the iconic DRCE. (Photo Courtesy Auto Imagery)

On stage at the NHRA Awards Ceremony, WJ delivered his championship speech with friend Linda Vaughn's lipstick kiss on his cheek. (Photo Courtesy Auto Imagery)

With the Oldsmobile partnership came enough funding to bring the operation to another level. The truck and trailer and WJ's Cutlass were part of a preseason photo shoot in Pomona in 1988.

By 2004, WJ was working on the third rendition of the DRCE and was designing a block that would lend itself to higher RPM with a stabilized valvetrain. The DRCE-3 was approximately 48 pounds heavier than the DRCE-2, so it required what WJ called "a lightening operation."

The next iteration brought about the DRCE-4 with a cylinder head that WJ designed shortly after the DRCE-3 was complete.

WJ stands over the engine compartment, just thinking.

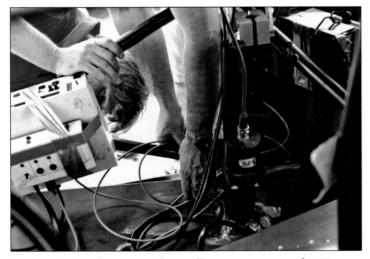

Testing in Bradenton and installing a computer for Firestone Tires. This was in the early portion of his career, but it was just another way that WJ was involved in research and development outside of just the engine compartment.

"The DRCE-3 was probably the most significantly different from the rest," said WJ. "That engine involved the biggest changes, and the DRCE-4 was just tidying up a few little things. The real advantage to the DRCE-4 is that it has decent material in it. [GM] went to a foundry in England called Grainger & Worrall, and that's where basically all ferrous blocks are cast. They cast Ford and GM NASCAR blocks there, and it's really the Cadillac of foundries. Their work is absolutely impeccable."

According to WJ, the DRCE-2 has been the engine most used in NHRA Pro Stock competition.

"A lot of people tend to stick to that one just because they've worked with it for so long," he explained. "They feel more comfortable with it than they do the DRCE-3, which has a lot more potential. It's just that they were competitive with what they had, and people don't like change.

"You have to realize that if you were to change, you would have to do R&D [research and development], and that would cost money. From a financial standpoint, if I'm winning with what I've got, why move to something—even if it's potentially better? That's a false sense of security though. Somebody else will eventually figure out the better mousetrap, and they will beat them with it."

Fiercely focused, supremely methodical, and incredibly precise, WJ seemed to work contentedly in solitude most of his life. Part of his success, however, has been admitting that one man can only do so much. WJ wasn't out taking polls or calling friends for advice, but one person he does recall working with on the development of the original DRCE was Larry Olson from Engine Prototype Development in Nevada.

"I'd known Larry since forever," said WJ. "He helped me with roughing-in all these parts, and he volunteered a lot of his time to help get this thing off the ground. He physically created core boxes and things like that, and he was a big help. I was born handicapped; I only have two hands. Sometimes you have to ask for help."

The Extra Set of Hands

WJ and Larry Olson had been friends since their racing paths crossed in the early 1970s.

An Exclamation Point

Though somewhat delayed, WJ's debut of the DRCE in 1983 was instantly gratifying. He was low qualifier in Baton Rouge at the Cajun Nationals and closed out the season with a victory in his powerful Hurts/Olds, thundering to a 7.65-second pass at 180 mph to oust defending world champion Lee Shepherd. Shepherd claimed the championship that year, but Johnson made a monumental move toward etching his name in Pro Stock history.

Oldsmobile in Action magazine, Vol. 1, 1984, claimed: "With the less-desirable features of the big-block Chevrolet motor eliminated and a host of competition-proven improvements built-in, Oldsmobile's newest and most powerful Rocket—now known as the Olds DRCE (Drag Racing Competition Engine)—comes very close to being a bulletproof piece."

"We just got along," said Olson, who was in the early stages of building his cylinder-head business at the time and quickly became accepted as part of the small team. "He could have done what I did. I was just the next pair of hands that actually had a brain—and I was one of the few people he trusted.

"We were both starting out. He'd stay on my fold-out coach when he raced in Southern California, and I'd stay at his house in Minnesota when we raced on the East Coast. I went to the races with him quite a lot, as much as I could. We were always in development, but a lot of times I didn't work on cylinder heads at all. I'd change tires, work on the clutch, mend the body when it would shake apart. You learn by being at the racetrack and helping tune on a car, and it's great for business, even if you're not doing anything but changing tires for the world champion. Everybody goes, 'Well, you can't be that stupid if you're working on that car.'"

Olson explained that during his time racing and collaborating with WJ, they worked on numerous projects that they designed together, created, and then tested on WJ's car.

"They all worked," said Olson.

When Oldsmobile's DRCE plans began to take shape, Olson was there. He was as eager to be part of the process as anyone would have been.

"We were at Orange County Raceway when Warren finally got the authorization to run the Oldsmobile," recalled Olson, who had moved from Southern California to Nevada and had a shop from which he supplied cylinder heads for many of the GM race cars in the NHRA, as well as the good majority of cars racing in the IHRA program.

"We came to my shop and started creating a cylinder head, and we physically made a cylinder head out of wood with ports and all the other things. It was far superior to any of the GM heads. We knew the fallacies and problems with the [previous engines]—some were bolt-hole location, some were mechanical things. We got the original head developed and flowed the wooden mock-up, and Warren took it over to a casting house. We took our wooden mock-up and sliced it into sections, put spacers in it, and used it to cast real cylinder heads. We literally did almost a freehand design, the very first ones."

Olson said he and WJ were generally on the same page with port sizing, flow numbers, and what they needed to win races. He would do the work, send it to WJ for review and to verify that they were in agreement, and together they would go from there.

"I thoroughly enjoyed racing with Warren and all of the development that we did together," said Olson. "We developed a lot of things and learned a lot from each other. He would send me his thoughts, and some of the first things I developed, he would run on his car. Whatever we did, I would keep it in my memory bank because he was my lead guy, my confidant. We developed and tested new things, and he was always a year ahead of what I had in my product line."

Trust was equal in their working relationship. When things didn't go so well, WJ did not blame Olson, and he never questioned his loyalty or discretion, although he easily could have because Olson also supplied cylinder heads to the competition, including the Dodge Boys and Bob Glidden.

"We had an unwritten agreement that he simply got it first," said Olson. "Good or bad, he got it first. He'd try it, and if it wasn't right, we'd fix it. We just solved problems. It was not uncommon for me to tape two handles to a box of cylinder heads, put them in the luggage bin on the airplane, and show up on his doorstep ready to install them.

"You can see in Warren's work that he loves the sport and how it allows you to express your creativity; you can see it in all the things he did. I created a single part on the car, but Warren did the whole thing, front to rear. He is a smart guy, hardheaded, talented, and a workaholic who's hard to keep up with. I was lucky to know him during the thin times when it all started for both of us. It was a blur, but it was sure fun."

CHAPTER 6

MAGNIFICENT MILESTONES

"The Professor of Pro Stock" comes by the moniker honestly. From the early days, he methodically chipped away at the Pro Stock stone to reveal an engineer's masterpiece. Cerebral and unwaveringly focused, Warren Johnson put forth tireless and consistent effort and was rewarded with extraordinary performance results that came with appropriate accolades.

On July 22, 2001, at Bandimere Speedway's Mopar Parts Mile-High Nationals, WJ surpassed rival Bob Glidden's 85 victories to become the most-winning Pro Stock driver in the history in the class.

Then 58 years old, WJ was en route to what would be his sixth NHRA Pro Stock championship. His final-round victory over son KJ at the Denver-area facility moved him ahead of Glidden on the all-time list. It was an almost unfathomable accomplishment, but WJ had few words.

"I would have to say it's been a pretty good day," said WJ at the conclusion of the event. "The driver was average, but the car was consistent. That's what you need to win these things."

He qualified his GM Goodwrench Service Plus Pontiac in the No. 3 position with a 7.283-second pass that was complemented by a track speed record of 189.71 mph. Then, he headed into Sunday eliminations, where

he defeated Mark Pawuk, V. Gaines, and Mike Edwards. In the final, WJ squared off with KJ in their 13th father-and-son final round. Well-tuned across the board, WJ had been first to leave the starting line all day long, and in the final he used a holeshot to send his only child away empty-handed, 7.347 to a quicker 7.335.

Two decades after passing Glidden's record, WJ continued to hold his position as the most prolific Pro Stock driver in NHRA history, ultimately extending his win total to 97, but he still had very little to say about it.

"The goal was to win races," said WJ. "If I lost, I would go back and analyze what I did wrong. If I won, I would go back and analyze what I did right and what the other guy did wrong. I never spent any time thinking about becoming the most winning driver or even staying that way."

In 2006, then wheeling the GM Performance Parts Pontiac GTO, WJ crossed the threshold of 500 career starts at The Strip at Las Vegas Motor Speedway. It went without much fanfare for such a bold testament to the longevity of his career.

GM Racing presented WJ with a plaque at Bandimere Speedway. It read: "Presented to Warren Johnson, Highest Honors to the "Professor of Pro Stock" for your lifetime achievement in the science of acceleration. Congratulations on becoming the Pro Stock driver with the most wins in NHRA history. We're very proud to have you on our team." The plaque was endorsed by Lynn Myers, General Manager, Pontiac-GMC Division, General Motors Corporation; and John Smith, Vice President, General Manager, GM Service Parts Operations. (Photo Courtesy Auto Imagery)

WJ and Larry Dixon are shown in the winner's circle after winning at Bandimere Speedway in 2001. It was WJ's 86th NHRA Pro Stock trophy, which edged him ahead of Bob Glidden as the most winning driver in the category. Dixon's own victory there was significant, as it marked the first Denver trophy for team owner Don "the Snake" Prudhomme. (Photo Courtesy Auto Imagery)

At the time of the event (the second-to-last race of the season), WJ had 96 NHRA national event wins, had reached 149 final rounds, and was at the top of nearly every performance list. The Professor had qualified No. 1 at 136 races, the most of anyone in any class, and had set top speed 206 times.

On the way to that 500th race, Johnson rocketed past a plethora of mile markers.

The Race for Speed

WJ is not a prideful man. It isn't so much that he's exceptionally modest; he just doesn't consider much of anything to be a big deal. As a matter of fact, by nature, the venerable drag racer could never be considered overly emotional or expressive. He envisioned a goal and simply set out to achieve it, and although sometimes he experienced frustration with the outcome, it was generally short-lived. The other side of the coin is that when there was a time to celebrate, that was generally short-lived as well. There was always the next race to consider, one way or the other.

In any form of drag racing, horsepower is the name of the game; it's what makes the car go, what is consistently in demand, and what is most difficult to harness. In Pro Stock, a class that demands refined mechanical precision, horsepower is the most valuable of diamonds, deeply buried and only fully unearthed by the very best miners. There is no better example of horsepower than speed, and Johnson proved quite adept at excavating that particular gem.

After breaking the 180-mph speed barrier at the Golden Gate Nationals at Fremont Dragstrip in 1982

The 2003 season came with a perfect four wins in four final rounds for WJ. "A race car is just an inanimate object," he said. "It responds to what you do to it. If you lose, it's because you haven't turned the right dials or pressed the right buttons." (Photo Courtesy Auto Imagery)

with his 181.08 in qualifying, it was business as usual for the Professor. He finished what he set out to do by claiming the trophy in a final-round defeat of Shepherd. It was Johnson's 3rd career NHRA win in his 45th race.

Four years later, he was the driver to burst through the next major Pro Stock speed target, and he did it during qualifying for the most prestigious and biggest race on the NHRA tour: the U.S. Nationals at Indianapolis.

WJ's Oldsmobile Firenza was a well-oiled machine in qualifying for Indy in 1986, and that allowed the Professor to take full advantage of mineshaft conditions during qualifying. His efforts introduced the class to the 190s, and it was a full year before anyone else could better his record-blasting 190.07-mph pass. Bob Glidden reset the record at 191.32 the next year at the same event.

In Las Vegas in 2006, WJ became the first professional NHRA competitor to race in 500 national events. By the conclusion of his career, he had competed in 649 NHRA Pro Stock races with a win-loss record of 874-507. (Photo Courtesy Auto Imagery)

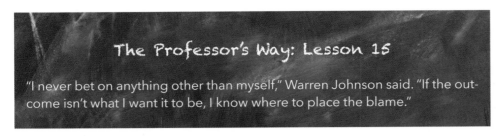

The Professor's Way: Lesson 15

"I never bet on anything other than myself," Warren Johnson said. "If the outcome isn't what I want it to be, I know where to place the blame."

The 1982 season proved to be a very good year for WJ. He defeated Lee Shepherd in the final round at the Summernationals in Englishtown to claim his first NHRA Pro Stock win, and in October he drove the same Oldsmobile Starfire to a 181.08-mph pass to burst through the previously impenetrable barrier that held the class back from exceeding 180. (Photo Courtesy Auto Imagery)

Just a member of the crew back in those days, Greg Anderson stands behind WJ's Firenza at a test session at Moroso Motorsports Park. WJ debuted the Firenza in 1986. "The competition only came into play because I had to make a living at it, but the development and being creative, that was my real interest in racing," said WJ.

In 1990, WJ recaptured the record going 192.18 in Dallas. It was less than 1 mph faster, but the small step continued the progress toward the next target: 200 mph.

The record for speed was reset 13 times between WJ's 190.07 and the big 200, and 9 of those marked points belonged to the Professor. The only other drivers able to pen their names on the list of national records for speed during that period were Bob Glidden (193.21 mph, Sonoma 1991) and Darrell Alderman (196.59 mph, Houston 1994).

Breaking the Double Century Mark

On April 25, 1997, during Friday night qualifying at Virginia Motorsports Park outside Richmond, Virginia, WJ had all of the right pieces in place to again mark his place in history—this time with a monumental, unforgettable, and undeniably impactful achievement.

In the lanes before making the pass, WJ was cautiously optimistic.

"Well, everyone out here is trying," he said. "Whether we accomplish it or not will just depend on who has the proper setup for the conditions out here. I'm sure you'll see a couple of 199s."

National Dragster Senior Editor Kevin McKenna was following the trail to 200 mph closely and was among those in attendance at the Richmond event when the coveted number finally came up on the scoreboard.

"It was a big deal; I think all of 1997 everyone knew it was coming," recalled McKenna. "WJ set the national record in Gainesville at 199.91, and you can almost hear the crowd groaning even now. You just knew it was going to happen, and WJ was all over it, setting top speed at every race. Unless something really unusual happened, he was going to be the guy."

WJ and Joe Lepone Jr. raced one another in qualifying at the U.S. Nationals in 1986. Although Lepone was a worthy competitor, the two never had the opportunity to square off in a final round. (Photo Courtesy Auto Imagery)

In 1986 and 1987, the years WJ drove the GM Goodwrench-branded Firenza, he picked up a total of six wins and four No. 1-qualifier awards.

McKenna could have watched from the pressroom, but the air was prickly with anticipation, and sitting still on the cusp of one of drag racing's greatest milestones wasn't a realistic option. The seasoned reporter took his place in front of the tower on the left side of the track to watch from behind the waterbox.

WJ staged next to fellow engine builder and veteran Pro Stock racer Steve Schmidt, and the two launched with wheels up. Schmidt was slightly ahead at the 60-foot marker, but WJ made up time with hyperefficiency. He was more than a hundredth ahead by the time the pair passed the eighth mile, where Johnson was already at 159.34 mph.

In front of a live television audience and in well-aligned atmospheric and track conditions, WJ crossed the finish-line stripe in his GM Performance Parts Pontiac with a 6.894-second pass at 200.13 mph. The pass reset both ends of the national record.

"Everybody watched that run," said McKenna. "Every crew guy from every team was on the starting line, and the crowd reaction was huge. I think everyone knew the conditions were as good as they were going to get, and sure enough, it happened. We didn't get another 200-mph run the whole year."

In the pits with the Firenza at Brainerd in 1986. WJ stands with his nephew Ragen, KJ, and Gary Stinnett (inside the car). Stinnett worked with the team for a short time. He is a multi-time NHRA Sportsman champion in the Super Comp category and claimed his 25th national event win in 2019. "I hope that everyone who has come through here over the years has learned something that they can take and apply to what they do in the future," said WJ. "That's why people referred to this place as WJ University."

Buzzy Woitas from WJ's crew, Kurt, Gene Stinnett (crew-member Gary Stinnett's father), and Pro Stock competitor Butch Leal stand in the Team Oldsmobile pit area at the U.S. Nationals in 1986.

WJ races his Firenza against Bob Morton in the Cooper & Kreigh Chevrolet at Brainerd International Raceway in 1986. (Photo Courtesy Auto Imagery)

At the top end, WJ emerged from his Pro Stocker smiling and reaching to shake the extended hands of everyone crowding around with congratulations.

"What a relief," he said, breathless and beaming. "I tell you, everyone has been trying to do this. We always had the fear somebody was going to get one good run in ahead of us. Man, I tell you. This is a relief. Kurt first in the 6s, me in the 200s. We're happy."

Then–Crew Chief Greg Anderson was equally as joyful at the starting line, proclaiming, "We're on top of the world. It's been so hard to do that. You have to have the perfect conditions. It's probably the only shot we're going to get all year, and we made a perfect run. It was perfect."

That weekend at Virginia Motorsports Park was magic for WJ, and a culmination of many years of hard work and relentless dedication to his craft. After qualifying concluded, WJ remained the No. 1 qualifier in what was then the quickest field in NHRA Pro Stock history. The Professor dominated among the 31 cars vying for a spot in the 16-car field with his record-smashing pass and historic 200-mph run, and he rode the wave into race day.

WJ reset the records again in the first round, going 6.883 at 200.53 mph in his defeat of Mike Thomas's 6.97 at 197 mph. Jerry Eckman was a no-show in the quarter-finals, and WJ put a 6.98 at 198 mph on the board to advance to the semifinals, where he met up with longtime adversary Darrell Alderman. WJ's 6.93 at 198 mph handily defeated his opponent's 6.99 at 195 mph and came with a ticket to the 100th final round of his career, the most of any other

When WJ rocketed to a 200.13-mph pass at Virginia Motorsports Park in 1997, drag racing historians labeled the achievement as the last of the six major performance milestones in the NHRA's four-wheeled professional categories. His 6.894-second ET was also the quickest in history and the first time that a Pro Stock car had gone quicker than 6.90. "That Firebird was not very aerodynamic, and it was big," WJ said. "But that was what I had to work with, and you make do with what you've got. I massaged that car plenty, and it was pretty efficient for a Firebird. If I would have had the Firenza back then, it probably would have happened five years sooner." (Art Courtesy Matt Levonas)

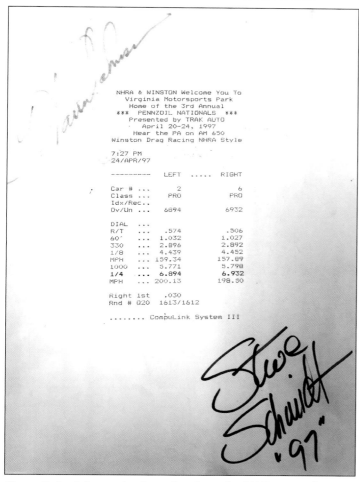

NHRA & WINSTON Welcome You To
Virginia Motorsports Park
Home of the 3rd Annual
*** PENNZOIL NATIONALS ***
Presented by TRAK AUTO
April 20-24, 1997
Hear the PA on AM 650
Winston Drag Racing NHRA Style

7:27 PM
24/APR/97

--------- LEFT ..... RIGHT

Car # ...   2   6
Class ...   PRO   PRO
Idx/Rec..
Ov/Un ...   6894   6932

DIAL ...
R/T 574   .506
60' ...   1.032   1.027
330 ...   2.896   2.892
1/8 ...   4.439   4.452
MPH ... 159.34   157.89
1000 ...   5.771   5.798
1/4 ...   6.894   6.932
MPH ... 200.13   198.50

Right 1st   .030
Rnd # 020 1613/1612

.... CompuLink System III

Steve Schmidt was in the other lane for WJ's record-busting pass. Both racers signed a copy of the timeslip that resides in Arlene Johnson's scrapbook.

then-active driver. There, he emerged victorious over son KJ, who suffered a broken transmission and watched as his father earned the trophy on a 6.95 at 198 mph.

In addition to the event trophy, WJ's spoils from the Richmond event included a $25,000 payout for becom-

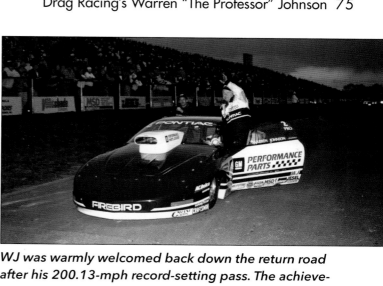

WJ was warmly welcomed back down the return road after his 200.13-mph record-setting pass. The achievement was one that he held in high regard, but there was no large party afterward. "We didn't celebrate much," admitted WJ. "Everybody in the pits knew it was going to happen sooner or later; we were just the fortunate ones to do it. That was just something else that we accomplished. The real challenge was to win the race, and we did." (Photo Courtesy Auto Imagery)

ing the first member of the NHRA Speed-Pro 200-mph Pro Stock Club and $15,000 from the MBNA World Record Club for setting the elapsed-time mark.

"It wasn't significant because it was a milestone. It was significant to me because I was determined enough to do it, able to tap into all the technology that's out there, and able to apply it to what I was doing," said WJ 23 years later. "That's what stands out for me more than anything."

For a 30-year period beginning with the 1973 season (the year that the NHRA began recording Pro Stock national performance records), WJ reset either one or both ends of the record on 29 occasions. His son, KJ, accomplished the goal four times.

The record for elapsed time (ET) was reset 80 times over those three decades by 23 different drivers. WJ did it 11 times.

The record for speed was reset 63 times and by 19 different drivers. WJ did it 24 times.

There were 20 occasions in which both the ET and speed records got a pummeling, and that double-up reset was handled by 8 different drivers. WJ accomplished the feat 7 times, and he was the only driver to do it from 1993 all the way until 2001, when KJ stepped in to get the job done.

When the scoreboard lit up with a 6.894 at 200.13 mph, the crowd roared in approval. "Just think about it," said WJ. "You're at 200 mph and want to go 201. What's it going to take? You have to look at everything, and I mean everything. I was fanatic about car preparation, but this was a case of right place, right time, right equipment." (Photo Courtesy Auto Imagery)

Warren Johnson Racing's History of NHRA National Performance Records				
Year	Month	Location	Driver	Record
1976	May	Denver, Colorado	WJ	156.66 mph
1976	June	Marion, South Dakota	WJ	157.78 mph
1976	July	Englishtown, New Jersey	WJ	158.45 mph
1976	August	Montreal, Canada	WJ	158.73 mph
1982	September	Indianapolis, Indiana	WJ	179.28 mph
1982	October	Fremont, California	WJ	181.08 mph (first to 180 mph)
1984	March	Gainesville, Florida	WJ	182.55 mph
1986	September	Indianapolis, Indiana	WJ	190.07 mph (first to 190 mph)
1988	October	Houston, Texas	WJ	7.282 seconds
1990	October	Dallas, Texas	WJ	192.18 mph
1991	September	Reading, Pennsylvania	WJ	7.180 seconds
1992	March	Houston, Texas	WJ	193.38 mph
1992	March	Gainesville, Florida	WJ	194.46 mph
1992	August	Sonoma, California	WJ	194.51 mph
1993	March	Houston, Texas	WJ	7.027 seconds, 195.05 mph
1993	March	Gainesville, Florida	WJ	196.24 mph
1994	April	Atlanta, Georgia	WJ	197.15 mph
1994	May	Englishtown, New Jersey	KJ	6.988 seconds (first in the 6s)
1995	March	Houston, Texas	WJ	6.948 seconds, 199.15 mph
1997	February	Pomona, California 1	WJ	6.927 seconds
1997	March	Gainesville, Florida	WJ	199.91 mph
1997	April	Richmond, Virginia	WJ	6.883 seconds, 200.53 mph (first to 200 mph)
1998	March	Gainesville, Florida	WJ	6.873 seconds, 201.20 mph
1998	October	Dallas, Texas 2	WJ	6.867 seconds, 201.34 mph
1999	March	Gainesville, Florida	WJ	6.866 seconds, 201.37 mph
1999	May	Richmond, Virginia	KJ	6.840 seconds
1999	May	Richmond, Virginia	WJ	202.24 mph
1999	October	Dallas, Texas 2	WJ	6.822 seconds, 202.33 mph
1999	October	Houston, Texas 2	WJ	202.36 mph
2001	September	Chicago, Illinois 2	KJ	6.801 seconds, 202.70 mph
2003	February	Pomona, California 1	WJ	204.91 mph
2003	April	Houston, Texas	WJ	6.720 seconds
2003	April	Houston, Texas	KJ	205.57 mph

The NHRA began tracking national records in 1973.

Crew Chief of the Race honors went to Greg Anderson for WJ's Winternationals performance in 1997. WJ set a new national record at 6.927 in his Pontiac Firebird and won the event with a final-round defeat of KJ. It was WJ's first national record for GM's Pontiac brand after so many years in an Oldsmobile.

"Setting top speed and national records was just a product of trying to be as competitive as possible," explained WJ. "I learned how to make cars run, and we had more speed than most people because my cars were efficient. Others would put a motor in it and tires on it and they were good to go, but that's not the way it was. I worked on every aspect of that car, from the most minute detail, right down to the wheel bearings, to determine what could make it more efficient. But I found it enjoyable. Taking that approach allowed me to educate myself on a lot of things that could bear fruit in other areas."

Six-Second Shot

Three years before WJ moved the speed needle up and over the 200-mph mark, his son, KJ, wielded WJ horsepower to dip down into the 6-second range for the first time in the history of the class.

Frank Iaconio had been the first NHRA Pro Stock driver to say hello to the 7s, and he did so at the 1982 Winternationals in Pomona, California, with an astounding 7.822-second pass that decisively put Glidden's previous 8.23 record out to pasture. On May 20, 1994, at the Summernationals in Englishtown, New Jersey, 31-year-old KJ blasted down the quarter mile to a 6.988 to carve his own name in the book.

"I remember rolling into that race on Thursday, and it was cold, there was hail coming down, and we had high barometric pressure," recalled KJ. "If it would dry up, we knew somebody had a shot to run 6 seconds."

In the afternoon session, Dodge campaigners Darrell Alderman and Scott Geoffrion put down promising passes in the warmer air, but KJ and WJ both overpowered the racing surface. In the second session and in just the second pair out, Alderman matched the national record with a 7.027-second pass. There were 30-plus Pro Stock cars there to take a shot at securing their place in history, and KJ was biding his time.

"We'd made a terrible run the first session, but I was confident with what we had under the hood. I knew that if I got off to a good start and made a clean pass, there was a chance," said KJ, who was wheeling an Olds Cutlass at the time. "The session took about 40 minutes, but I waited until the end, until the air got absolutely the best it could get. When I let the clutch out, it had the wheels in the air, and it was a smooth run. It was absolutely flawless. Everybody was pitching their best, but I was the lucky one there."

By making the first sub-7-second run in the history of the class, KJ locked in the founder's position in Holley's 6-Second Club along with a $25,000 bonus. And because the Johnson family doesn't like to do anything halfway,

KJ went on to win the Pro Stock Budweiser Challenge for an additional $50,000.

He backed up the national record with a 7.03 in the final of the bonus race to pocket $7,500 from the Slick 50 World Record Club Bonus Fund. In all, including $5,500 earned for his semifinals finish in the main event and the $3,000 No. 1 qualifier bonus, KJ's winnings for the weekend were $91,000.

The younger Johnson held the national record until the Houston race the following season, when his father ran a 6.948.

"We were all focused on increasing the performance of our cars, no matter what we had to do. It was a product of everybody's efforts," said WJ. "It didn't matter which one of us got the record, as long as it was one of our cars. Everybody's hands were pulling in the same direction."

Father and Son Make History

WJ and KJ were always working toward the same goal: bringing home a victory for the team. They worked side by side both on and off the racetrack, knew exactly what the other had under the hood, and shared all of their accumulated data. More than just a family that raced together, they were very much a team on the NHRA tour.

In a career driven by incredible horsepower, WJ claimed 36 national records. He was the first to 180 mph, the first to 190, and the first to 200, and he set and reset track records all across the country. His fast race cars often were the catalyst to big paydays, as evidenced by this $25,000 check from Slick 50 for his 7.02 ET, the best of the weekend, clocked at the Winston Select Finals. (Photo Courtesy Auto Imagery)

KJ sits in the driver's seat in 1994, the year he broke into the 6-second zone in Pro Stock. It was just his second season driving a Pro Stock car.

Following in his father's footsteps, KJ claimed a major marker in the history of Pro Stock in 1994 when he became the first driver in the class to make a pass quicker than 7 seconds. KJ raced to a 6.988 at the Summernationals in English-town, on the very hallowed grounds where his father had claimed his first win. (Art Courtesy Matt Levonas)

The Professor's Way: Lesson 16

"I never targeted a performance goal; I targeted winning races," Warren Johnson said. "If you're going to be winning races, then you need to have a competitive car, and everything else has to be in the correct order. If you have that combination right, then the performance should be there."

Both were very driven to win, but they presented themselves as more of a single entity rather than two separate competitors. Because the two possessed the same amount of power and had equal access to resources, the stage was set for a unique opportunity in NHRA drag racing.

KJ made his NHRA debut at the Pomona Winternationals in 1993, and it only took five races before he reached his first Pro Stock final round. At Atlanta Dragway, just a stone's throw from home, KJ found himself face-to-face in the final with his father. It was the first father-son final round in NHRA history.

"Anytime we went to a race, we were thoroughly convinced that we had the potential to win that race with either of our cars," said WJ. "We knew it would hap-pen eventually. We just had no idea which of us would end up on top. I consider Kurt the better driver."

WJ got the win light that day at the Southern Nationals: 7.179 at 193.05 mph to 7.226 at 193.00 mph. He sent his son away empty-handed twice more before a very persistent KJ was able to garner some retribution with a final-round defeat of dear ole dad at Maple Grove Raceway that same year.

In that first season of KJ's Pro Stock driving career, the two went to battle in the money round six times with father hoisting the trophy on four of those occasions. Notably, KJ, the NHRA Rookie of the Year, finished second in Pro Stock points to WJ, thereby etching another note in the history book as the first father and son to do so.

The two raced against one another in a total of 13 final rounds between 1993 and 2001 at a variety of race-tracks across the country. Location didn't seem to matter much when it came to a particular facility's likelihood of hosting the father-son duel; the only track with repeat

The 1993 season was productive for WJ. KJ made his Pro Stock debut and was struck by immediate success as well as challenge. The two had the opportunity to race against one another and make history, and the season was capped by a championship title, WJ's second in a row. (Photo Courtesy Auto Imagery)

WJ and KJ raced many times in eliminations, not just in the final round. Here they are squaring off in the semifinals at Bristol Dragway in 2005. Warren recorded a 0.025-second reaction time to Kurt's 0.039, and they raced down the quarter mile with incredibly evenly matched race cars. WJ got the nod at the stripe with his 6.757-second pass at 204.29 mph to his son's 6.759 at 204.05 mph. WJ, who clocked low ET of the event in round two with a 6.715 went on to raise the trophy after a final-round defeat of Richie Stevens Jr. (Photo Courtesy Auto Imagery)

KJ (near lane) and WJ perform side-by-side burnouts ahead of making a qualifying pass at the U.S. Nationals in 2013. With almost no funding, the Johnson team raced a limited season in 2013. WJ competed in 10 events, and KJ raced in 12. (Photo Courtesy Auto Imagery)

Johnson-versus-Johnson finals was the venerable Maple Grove in Reading, Pennsylvania.

"I don't think there were ever any hard feelings," said WJ. "I won and he didn't some of the time, and there were other situations where he won and I didn't. It was a case of knowing that one of us would win and one would lose. If you lose, you learn from it and try to win the next one."

A win for KJ was a win for the team. The younger Johnson's 40 national event wins were all claimed with Warren Johnson horsepower generated in the shop where they worked side by side. "When he became a driver, it didn't really change our relationship," said WJ. "We were both out there with cars that we felt were competitive enough to win, and it didn't make a difference to me which car won. Were we competitive against one another? Only when we ran each other." (Photo Courtesy Auto Imagery)

The Final Say

This chart shows how Warren Johnson and Kurt Johnson fared against each other in NHRA final rounds.

WJ claimed 10 of his 97 national event wins in a final-round dispute with son, KJ. (Photo Courtesy Auto Imagery)

Year	Location	Result
1993	Atlanta, Georgia	WJ def. KJ
1993	Englishtown, New Jersey	WJ def. KJ
1993	Columbus, Ohio	WJ def. KJ
1993	Reading, Pennsylvania	KJ def. WJ
1993	Dallas, Texas	KJ def. WJ
1993	Pomona, California 2	WJ def. KJ
1997	Pomona, California 1	WJ def. KJ
1997	Richmond, Virginia	WJ def. KJ
1998	Seattle, Washington	WJ def. KJ
1998	Memphis, Tennessee	WJ def. KJ
1999	Gainesville, Florida	WJ def. KJ
2000	Reading, Pennsylvania	KJ def. WJ
2001	Denver, Colorado	WJ def. KJ

CHAPTER 7

DOMINATION IN THE 1990s

Over the course of his first 19 years in the drag racing business, Warren Johnson established himself as a strong player in the game. The 1970s and 1980s were extraordinary. From his first start at the Indianapolis U.S. Nationals in 1971 until the final race of the 1989 NHRA season, he accumulated 20 national event wins in 144 races and 22 low qualifier awards.

Thanks to that hefty harvest, WJ closed out the 1980s riding high on eight consecutive top 5 finishes in the Pro Stock standings. He had been second in the world five times, brushing right up against the series championship. In hindsight, it is plain to see that the fiercely dedicated driver had methodically poured a foundation on which to build a legacy.

With two IHRA championships in the books, WJ was confident that he could challenge for an NHRA season trophy. With three wins in four final rounds for the 1982 season, he was showing proof that he was a contender. It took a decade from there to finally bring home an NHRA Drag Racing Series championship, but that gigantic accomplishment launched WJ into the most successful decade of his career.

"We knew that if we did everything right, we could be competitive enough and do it," WJ said of becoming a world champion. "But we certainly had to work for it. We didn't buy our first CNC machine until the end of 1992, and before that, you had to build all of those heads by hand. We used a Bridgeport and hand grinders to build 22 sets of heads in one year. That was research and development; it was just what you had to do to become more competitive."

Darrell Alderman earned the first two season championships of the decade for Dodge, claiming the title in 1990 and 1991. WJ, though, wasn't sitting idle and watching his rival steal the spotlight, nor was he pout-

Elbow grease wasn't something WJ ever shied away from. He always enjoyed working on his race cars more than driving them, but he wouldn't consider stepping out of the driver's seat. "Why would I hire a driver? I could make the same mistakes without having to pay anyone. I was in this deal to make a living. I wasn't out there to make somebody famous."

ing in a corner. The Professor was relentlessly striving for gains that he rightfully believed would pay off.

In 1990, WJ earned the victory over Bruce Allen in Houston and reached two other final rounds (Atlanta and Denver), both of which he forfeited to Larry Morgan. However, WJ was clearly chipping away and making horsepower gains. The proof was shown in six No. 1 qualifiers and a brand-new national record for speed (192.18 mph) in Dallas at Texas Motorplex.

Closing the season No. 5 in the nation wasn't up to par for WJ though. He greeted his 1991 campaign locked and loaded.

Bringing in Scott Geoffrion as a research and development driver in a second car shifted the team's education and growth into high gear. According to the Professor, expanding the team with a second car didn't have to do with anything other than gathering more information. Although they didn't discover anything groundbreaking during Scott's short tenure with the team, the additional data translated to more round wins overall.

The Professor's Way: Lesson 17

"I always went to a race with the confidence that we had a good enough package to win," Warren Johnson said. "If you've done your work, you can have that confidence. As for qualifying No. 1, well I looked at that as strictly a financial reward because it paid $3,000 extra. We went to the race to win, but you were that much better off if you could get that bonus."

The ACDelco Oldsmobile crosses the finish line in 1992 on the way to WJ's first NHRA Pro Stock championship. "It was a relatively successful period, as far as the racing operation was concerned," said WJ. It was his fifth year piloting the Cutlass body. (Photo Courtesy Les Welch Family)

The 1991 season included victory at the NHRA Winston Invitational in Rockingham, North Carolina, for WJ, who defeated Bob Glidden in the final of the bonus event. (Photo Courtesy Les Welch Family)

The crew in 1991 on top of the hauler sends its greetings to Arlene from above. From left to right are Buzzy Woitas, Ray Prince, and Pat Barrett. Buzzy was a longtime friend, Prince worked off and on with the Johnsons for a decade, and Barrett had been a friend and then crewmember dating all the way back to the late 1960s.

The 1990s were phenomenal for WJ in terms of horsepower gains, and it showed with a total of 95 No. 1-qualifier awards from 1990 to 1999. It also meant an increase in income, as every low qualifier award came with a tidy payday. (Photo Courtesy Les Welch Family)

Insider Perspective

"People who only know of Warren are intimidated, but once they meet him in person, they can see he's just a normal person. He's intense when he's working, and sometimes he won't talk if he's busy doing something, but most times, if there's a subject to talk about, he'll chat like anybody else."

– Arlene Johnson

"He was always there if I had questions, but he would let me go off on my own. He still does. We work in the same shop, but we have days where we don't talk. If I have questions, I ask—but other than that, he sets me free. I don't need somebody over my shoulder, and neither does he. It's always been like that, even with employees. If they have a question, they'll ask. But he's not there to hold your hand."

– Kurt Johnson

"Scott was a good enough driver that you could believe his input on what he experienced during the run," explained WJ. "Having him there was strictly a case of collecting more information, and it was really quite effective."

WJ was a finalist at the Pomona season opener, then again in Phoenix. Houston was the next race on tour, and there Geoffrion reached the final round in the ACDelco Olds Cutlass. Alderman was on the winning end of each of those first three battles of the season, but WJ emerged victorious over the defending champ at race four, snatching the trophy in the final second of the Gatornationals in Gainesville, Florida.

The Gainesville victory marked

A rambunctious group of friends: (from left to right) Scott Geoffrion, "Big Dave" Cobert, KJ, and "Jim O" Jim Oberhofer. Although relatively even-keeled, just like his father, KJ kept entertaining company over the years.

the first of four consecutive finals for WJ, as he and Alderman waged an early war for the points lead.

In the end, Alderman earned a second consecutive series title by putting his Dodge Daytona in the final round in all but three of the events on the schedule. The Mopar campaigner claimed 11 of the 18 trophies up for grabs, having to go through WJ four times to get the win.

Three of WJ's five trophies that season came with the defeat of Alderman. It was a brutal, season-long battle in which Alderman came out on top, but WJ's 5 wins in 11

The GM Performance Parts Olds in the staging lanes at Old Bridge Township Raceway Park. That's Pat Barrett giving it a nudge. WJ's first win came at the Englishtown, New Jersey, facility, and he won three other times there. (Photo Courtesy Evan J. Smith)

final rounds were complemented by 8 starts from the No. 1 spot, as well as a new national record of 7.180 seconds recorded in Reading, Pennsylvania.

WJ finished second in 1991, but he had most assuredly sounded an alarm that rang with annoying repetition in the back of his competitor's minds over the offseason.

Personal trouble for Alderman culminated in a temporary suspension from NHRA competition before the 1992 season, and their rivalry was put on hold. WJ's job, though, did not get any easier with the absence of that particular adversary.

Becoming the Champ

"Before the start of the season, we thought there would be six cars that could conceivably win the championship," said WJ to Steve Evans for *NHRA Today* in 1992. "We felt that if we could have two cars, that would improve our chances."

The curveball to the two-car formula was that test driver Geoffrion had been invited to take over the seat of

Engine Matters in the 1990s

WJ used the DRCE-1 until 1992, when he redesigned the cylinder head to make, as he said, "cosmetic improvements." In 1996, the DRCE-2 was updated with 4,900 bore spacing, and 1997 began the DRCE-3 redesign, which was not complete until the early 2000s.

Alderman's championship-winning Dodge for 1992. WJ considered Geoffrion a friend and encouraged him to do what was right for the growth of his career, and he genuinely wished him well, but the Professor was left with a bit of a conundrum. It was quickly resolved, though, with the addition of Don Beverley as the driver of the second car.

KJ was officially appointed as crew chief, and he enthusiastically stepped into the role for what he christened "Team II." He emerged that season as a man who could hold his own. He tuned Beverley to his first final in only their second race together, which was at Phoenix, and then guided his driver to a first win at Atlanta over Warren Johnson Racing teammate-turned-rival Geoffrion.

Just past the midway point of the season, Beverley met WJ for the first time in a final round, and Team II came away with the Denver win. The championship chase, however, had already turned in WJ's favor.

The season had started with a large statement from Jerry Eckman, who emerged from the cage of the offseason with fury and picked up the Winternationals win. He claimed victory again the following weekend at Phoenix, was runner-up to WJ in Gainesville, and then won Columbus.

"We weren't worried about Jerry though," WJ said. "We were worried about bringing our own program up to speed. We had a few glitches to iron out, but we came to Gainesville and were strong."

WJ's Gatornationals performance was shiny and bright as he threw down 7.14s all day on Sunday en route to the win. The gap was closed between WJ and Eckman with a win over Geoffrion in Memphis, and victory at

WJ's powerful DRCE produced a total of 138 No. 1–qualifier awards over the course of his career. In this image, he and Arlene, along with then-crewmembers Robert "Gordie" Gordon and Greg Anderson, pose for the photographers in 1992 with the oversized low qualifier check.

All the pretty maids in a row—or a bunch of camshafts, anyway—each representing a different way of working with the engine. The measuring device is the black piece in front. Johnson's extensive research and development, aided by an income that bloomed in direct relation to performance and winnings, brought many parts and pieces into his workshop. Most of what he acquired through the years still resides in his warehouse.

The clean and tidy rear end of one of WJ's early 1990s Olds Cutlass Pro Stockers. His first year in a Cutlass was 1988 after two successful seasons in the Firenza.

KJ held his own from an early age and was crew chief for Team II with Don Beverley as the driver in 1992. By 1993, he was in a car of his own.

KJ is on the starting line with Oldsmobile representative Eddie Bennett in Seattle in 1992, waiting for his driver, Don Beverley, to make a run. (Photo Courtesy Auto Imagery)

KJ was crew chief for Don Beverley, who drove a second car for the team in 1992. They won Denver over WJ and Atlanta over Scott Geoffrion that season. "There was a lot of conjecture from the press that it was one of those blocking programs, but it was never constructed that way," explained WJ. "It was a contract that there were no dives being taken by either car." (Photo Courtesy Auto Imagery)

When Don Beverley (left) drove the Team II Oldsmobile for Warren Johnson Racing in 1992, he brought home two wins for the team with KJ as crew chief: one in Atlanta over Scott Geoffrion, who was then driving for Dodge, and the other over WJ in Denver.

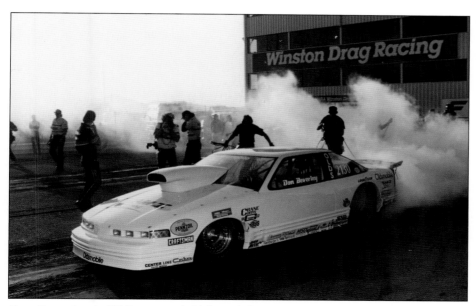

Don Beverley in WJ's second Oldsmobile Cutlass in 1992. (Photo Courtesy Auto Imagery)

Englishtown three races later really started the downhill snowball. WJ reached the final in Denver and then came away with the trophy in Sonoma, and an Indy win kicked off an impactful streak that would, ultimately, finalize the championship.

"Winning Indy gave us some kind of momentum that we hadn't really counted on," said WJ, a career six-time U.S. Nationals winner. "I don't know if we demoralized our competitors or what really happened, but we won three races in a row in a somewhat convincing fashion."

The Professor was victorious at Indy over Larry Morgan, at Reading over Eckman, and at Topeka over Geoffrion.

By the time WJ got to Texas Motorplex, all he had to do was qualify for the Dallas event in his ACDelco Olds Cutlass to lock down his first world championship. Leaving nothing to chance, he laid down a track record–setting 7.109-second pass to secure the top spot in what was then the quickest field in NHRA Pro Stock history. Jim Yates held down the bump spot with a 7.216.

For WJ, there was something of an asterisk on sewing up the championship in Dallas because he didn't win the race. WJ stated at the time that he had mixed emotions, but he finished the season with one last trophy and an optimistic outlook that would serve him well.

"We already had the championship going into Pomona, so we didn't look at winning the Finals as a good way to close 1992," he said. "We looked at it as a way to start 1993 with some momentum."

KJ stepped into the role of second driver for the team in 1993 with quite pleasing results. Although it was not altogether smooth sailing—a series of crashes for the rookie driver peppered a season of success—WJ's protégé established a bit of his own authority in the class. He took three wins in seven final rounds and was crowned Rookie of the Year by the NHRA.

The duo effectively held off Geoffrion, who finished third, and Larry Morgan, who emerged as an early threat but ultimately claimed a lone victory in six finals.

The year was one of the most glittery in all of WJ's career. He claimed his 50th No. 1–qualifier award and 75th top speed award, and he was crowned Pro Stock

KJ accepts the $1,000 check for being crew chief of the Race at the Denver Mile-High Nationals at Bandimere Speedway in 1992. KJ tuned Don Beverley to a final-round victory over WJ at the event. (Photo Courtesy Auto Imagery)

Johnson in the lanes, waiting to make a run. (Photo Courtesy Auto Imagery)

Pro Stock Motorcycle rider "Pizza" John Mafaro talks shop with WJ following a win in the 1990s.

This is the ACDelco Oldsmobile that won WJ's first NHRA championship in 1992. WJ won 6 total championships in NHRA Pro Stock—the second-most in the class to Bob Glidden's 10. WJ was tied at No. 6 on the all-time wins list in 2020, the year this book was written. John Force had 16 in Funny Car, Bob Glidden and Dave Schultz (Pro Stock Motorcycle) were tied with 10 each, Tony Schumacher had 8 Top Fuel titles, and Andrew Hines (Pro Stock Motorcycle) and Kenny Bernstein (2 in Top Fuel, 4 in Funny Car) had accumulated 6. (Photo Courtesy Les Welch Family)

No. 2 adorned the window of the 1992 Oldsmobile Cutlass, but WJ made hay when the sun was shining to score his first NHRA Pro Stock championship. He logged eight wins in nine final rounds and held a win-loss record of 48-10 in elimination rounds by season's end. (Photo Courtesy Auto Imagery)

Driver of the Year as part of the highly respected *Car Craft* All-Star Drag Racing Team.

WJ's 1993 championship came by way of an abundant total of 9 trophies obtained in 12 finals. Kurt was his biggest challenger—only 5 of 18 events that year were devoid of a Johnson in the final. The national standings, with WJ and KJ at the top by year's end, composed another note for NHRA history. It was the first time a father and son had concluded the season No. 1 and No. 2 in the points in any of the NHRA's professional categories.

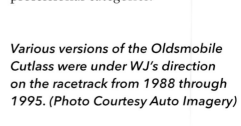

Various versions of the Oldsmobile Cutlass were under WJ's direction on the racetrack from 1988 through 1995. (Photo Courtesy Auto Imagery)

The top eight Pro Stockers in the country lined up on the track ahead of the Budweiser Challenge shoot-out at Old Bridge Township Raceway Park in Englishtown. The competition first began in 1985, and WJ raced for the special trophy 24 times. (Photo Courtesy Evan J. Smith)

WJ signs giveaway goodies at an ACDelco function in the mid-1990s.

Owning Indy

WJ took his first big bite out of the Granddaddy of them all, the Big Go, the U.S. Nationals at Indianapolis, when he won it in 1984. In the 1990s, he was nearly unstoppable when it came to Indy wins, and when he couldn't get to the final round, his son took care of business. A Warren Johnson–prepared Pro Stocker reached the Indy final each year from 1992–1999. Only one of those years did the team not bring a trophy back home to Sugar Hill, Georgia.

WJ beat Larry Morgan for the trophy in the Indy final in 1992, Scott Geoffrion in 1993, Mark Pawuk in 1994, and Lewis Worden in 1995. In the history of the event, only four drivers in any Pro category have won there four years in a row: WJ is joined on that exclusive list by Bob Glidden and Greg Anderson in Pro Stock and Tony Schumacher in Top Fuel.

The 1996 and 1997 trophies went to KJ, who displaced Rickie Smith and V. Gaines for the Indy title. In 1998, it was Mike Edwards with the win over WJ, who came back in 1999 to defeat former crew chief Greg Anderson for the U.S. Nationals victory.

The Professor's Way: Lesson 18

"I don't blame losing on anybody but myself," Warren Johnson said. "If I have control of all the assets here, it means I made a wrong decision someplace. If I was late in the lights, that's me. You think about it, but you don't talk about it to anybody else. I never let anything like that bother me. You don't accept losing because then you really are a loser. But you accept that you made the wrong decision in some area, and you need to fix it."

A thoughtful WJ is in the back of the pit area in 1992.

The Ascension

The 1992 and 1993 championships were hard-fought and satisfying, and 1994 brought its own magnificent reward when KJ made the first sub-7-second pass in NHRA Pro Stock history with a record-blasting 6.988-second ET in Englishtown. WJ horsepower was on display in Atlanta that year as well, when he reset the national top speed record at 197.15 mph.

Johnson finished No. 3 in 1994 behind the Dodge Boys: titlist Alderman and second-place Geoffrion

WJ earned the second of his six NHRA world championships in 1993, along with fellow Pro winners (front row from left to right): Dave Schultz (Pro Stock Motorcycle), WJ, John Force (Funny Car), and Eddie Hill (Top Fuel). Sportsman champions are (back row from left to right): Blaine Johnson, Randy Anderson, Bill Maropulos, Miss Winston Deb Brittsan, future Pro Stock racer Greg Stanfield, eventual three-time Pro Stock champion Jason Line, Scotty Richardson, and John Wood. (Photo Courtesy Auto Imagery)

A peek inside the race shop in Sugar Hill, Georgia, between events in 1994. KJ's Pro Stock Olds is closest to the photographer (Arlene) and facing his dad's No. 1 car. The race cars are parked between the front offices of Warren Johnson Enterprises and the back area where all of the machinery is housed.

WJ, near lane, raced Mark Pawuk at the Keystone Nationals with the No. 3 on his window, signifying his position in the standings at the conclusion of the 1994 season. That No. 3 was sandwiched between championships in 1993 and 1995. (Photo Courtesy of Evan J. Smith)

won 11 collective events. WJ won four of the seven final rounds he contested in a very trying season. Many of his competitors believed that something was amiss in the Dodge camp that season—something that didn't quite line up with the rule books and perhaps gave the first and second finishers an unfair advantage.

The Professor shook off any large concerns over his competitor's potential shenanigans and set his sights on the 1995 championship. Early on, the competition was fierce. The Dodge Boys won the first four races. Alderman reached one more final before it was reported that the Wayne County Speed Shop in Fairfield, Illinois, had been broken into by vandals, who destroyed their competitive blocks and cylinder heads. The legitimacy of the break-in raised eyebrows and brought much speculation, but the bottom line was that the two Dodge entries were unable to return for the remainder of the season.

"That is pretty low," said KJ, upon hearing of the destruction. "We know how we bust our butts. It takes us a month to prepare a block. Dad has one good motor, and my second best isn't up to his best. We basically have four motors, and if someone comes into our shop and steals them or destroys them, it wipes us out. It's no fun for us to win if we don't have anybody to race. It brings the level of competition down because it eliminates two of the top cars."

WJ observed the situation quietly and kept about his business, which never wavered from striving to win races. In Richmond, he returned to the winner's circle, which was immediately followed with a final round in Columbus, and another win in Topeka. KJ won the next event in Denver, and a runner-up for WJ in Sonoma was the precursor to four consecutive victories. He didn't make the final in either of the next two events but closed the season with a win in the NHRA Finals at Pomona and a third career NHRA championship.

WJ faced a variety of opponents throughout the 1995 season, including Mark Pawuk, Bob Glidden, Steve Schmidt, and Jim Yates, who were making their respective charge at the midseason mark. Yates was the biggest thorn in WJ's side as the second half wound down, repeatedly popping up to challenge him in final rounds and laying the groundwork for his own championship runs, which would take place in 1996 and 1997.

It was a second-place finish for Johnson in 1996,

The Horsepower Challenge

From 1985 until 2018, the top eight NHRA Pro Stock drivers competed in a once-yearly bonus event. The race within a race changed names over the years because a variety of manufacturers sponsored the event, but it was always the same basic format: eight drivers, three rounds, and one champion.

Warren Johnson earned a spot in the shoot-out in all but two years from 1985 until 2010. His 24 appearances stand out as the most of any driver in the history of the specialty race. WJ won the event in 1993 and 2002. Kurt Johnson made 16 appearances, and he earned the unique trophy in 1994 and 1998.

WJ is one of only nine drivers who won both the bonus and main events. He did so in 1993.

KJ's Olds Cutlass is shiny and waiting for its 1994 debut. KJ was winless that season, but he came back in 1995 and scored at least 1 win for 14 consecutive seasons.

The No. 1 car is ready for the 1994 season. After back-to-back championships in 1992 and 1993, WJ was prepared to go to battle again and emerge victorious. His four wins in seven final rounds left him relegated to third place. The Professor was back in form for 1995, though, when he claimed his third championship.

WJ reset both ends of the national record in Houston in 1995 with a 6.948-second pass at 199.15 mph and was rewarded by friends with this cake. It was the second official 6-second pass in history–KJ had broken into the 6s in Englishtown nearly a full year earlier. WJ's speed was almost 2 mph faster than Darrell Alderman's previous record that was set a year prior.

Loading up the race trailer for an event in 1995. WJ qualified for each event he attended in the 1990s, and he attended them all with his impressive Cutlass and then Firebird-bodied Oldsmobiles powered by the well-crafted DRCE.

Mike Edwards started racing in 1978 and worked his way up to Pro Stock. He procured a victory over WJ in 1998, his first over the Professor, three years after this photo was taken at Dallas in 1995. (Photo Courtesy Les Welch Family)

The 1990s were nonstop for WJ, who isn't exactly known for taking extended breaks to catch up on rest and relaxation.

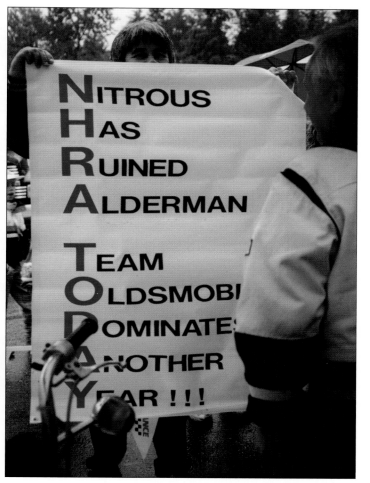

The Professor with Jill Caliendo McKenna, one of the first Jr. dragster competitors, in the staging lanes at Englishtown's Old Bridge Township Raceway Park in 1995. "If they had Jr. dragsters when I was a kid, they would have had wooden wheels," joked WJ. (Photo Courtesy Evan J. Smith)

Vocal fans showed their loyalty to WJ and the Oldsmobile team with a sign in the midst of the scandal involving the Wayne County Speed Shop and Darrell Alderman in 1995.

The GM Performance Parts Oldsmobile Cutlass in 1995, the year of WJ's third championship. "We had a mediocre driver, so we had to have the best-performing car," said WJ. His Olds was, indeed, a top performer, as he claimed 14 low-qualifier awards. (Photo Courtesy Les Welch Family)

In the pits in 1995. That championship season produced seven wins in nine final rounds, including victories in Richmond, Topeka, Seattle, Brainerd, Indianapolis, Reading, and at the NHRA Finals in Pomona.

Only Bob Glidden has more Pro Stock championships than WJ. In 1995, WJ wheeled the GM Performance Parts Oldsmobile Cutlass to his third of six overall championships. (Photo Courtesy Les Welch Family)

the seventh time he'd finished No. 2 in the nation, and along the way he logged the 75th No. 1–qualifier award of his career. Capping a fruitful season, he was again voted Pro Stock Driver of the Year in the *Car Craft* All-Star Drag Racing Team competition. In all, WJ was awarded the magazine's fan-voted title six times. He added another to the esteemed award list in 2001 as Pro Stock Engine Builder of the Year.

After a year of research and development with the Pontiac Firebird body, WJ left no doubt that he had found the sweet spot when he recorded the first 200-mph Pro Stock run. After doing so, the Professor plugged along, claiming a total of four wins in five final rounds to finish in the No. 2 position to Yates once more.

WJ was on top the following year in exceptional form. Over the winter, he had designed a new 5-speed clutchless transmission and developed a new cylinder head and intake manifolds. Then, he spent 16 straight hours in the GM wind tunnel testing the brand-new 1998 Firebird and a

Jim Yates (far lane) gave WJ a large challenge in the mid-1990s, claiming the championship in 1996 and 1997. (Photo Courtesy Les Welch Family)

The Pontiac Firebird piloted by WJ reached eight final rounds in 1996. He won five times and finished No. 2 in the nation to champion Jim Yates. "I didn't feel unstoppable. There's always some stone unturned, and that's the way I looked at it," said WJ. "I had to figure out what it's going to take to keep these things going quicker and faster, and it just happened to work out a little better in my favor in that decade." (Photo Courtesy Les Welch Family)

The move to the Pontiac Firebird in 1996 meant a new bodystyle to work with, and WJ dedicated himself to learning every nuance. Two years after debuting the Firebird, he claimed another championship. "Every championship was difficult to achieve," he said. "None of them were easy, none were a runaway. In fact, I think the first IHRA championship was won by 38 points. All that does is give you enough confidence that at least you're on the right path, and if you stick with it, you can continue to educate yourself every day to become better and better." (Photo Courtesy Evan J. Smith)

The 1996 Firebird wasn't primed for victory right out of the gate, but once the tour hit Richmond, WJ had found the formula. He won there and at Memphis, Topeka, Sonoma, Brainerd, and Reading. "I had a little bit of a learning curve with the Firebird," said WJ. "At the time, I had a Don Ness–built chassis, which had the stock 101-inch wheelbase, as compared to the Cutlass 107-inch wheelbase. The first time I drove it was in testing at Gainesville, and it felt like a really fast go-kart due to the difference in wheelbase. The aero balance was completely unlike the Cutlass. It took a little time to adapt to it all, but after a while it proved to be pretty successful." (Photo Courtesy Evan J. Smith)

Under new direction from GM at the conclusion of the 1995 season, WJ moved from the Oldsmobile Cutlass to the Pontiac Firebird. He was behind the wheel of a Firebird from 1996 until 2000 and won 27 times with that body with 48 low-qualifier awards as a keen complement. Two of his six championships came in that time period (1998 and 1999). (Photo Courtesy Auto Imagery)

Randy and Cindy Pruett of Shreveport, Louisiana, started out as fans and became friends to the Johnsons. They were huge supporters of the team and showed up to Dallas with T-shirts commemorating WJ's 200-mph pass. (Photo Courtesy Auto Imagery)

The cast and crew of the 1997 Dupont Automotive Finishes Pro Stock Challenge, a special race contested within a national event that was held from 1985 to 2018 under the banner of various sponsors. (Photo Courtesy Auto Imagery)

A rare photo of WJ (near lane) and Alderman at a match race at Atco Raceway in New Jersey in 1998. (Photo Courtesy Evan J. Smith)

WJ and his crew celebrate the 1999 U.S. Nationals win with the Superman-branded Pontiac Firebird. "It's our biggest race of the year and always has been," said WJ emphatically. "It's the Daytona 500 of drag racing. Everybody gears up for that race, parts-wise and mechanically, but mentally, you have to be prepared for it. I was fortunate to win it four years in a row, but I think you have to get in a mindset that you can win there. A lot of people think they can't win it, and that's the problem."

WJ is interviewed by Dave McClelland at the U.S. Nationals in 1999. Five of WJ's six Indy wins came in the 1990s, including his 1999 defeat of Greg Anderson at the most historic race on the tour. Winning Indy is an incredible badge of honor in NHRA competition, and only Bob Glidden had more Pro Stock wins (nine) at the venerable facility at the time of this writing. (Photo Courtesy Auto Imagery)

new Chevy Camaro for KJ.

In a repeat of his 1993 championship season, WJ was a powerhouse in 1998, racing to 9 victories in 12 final rounds and qualifying in the top spot 13 times in his squeaky new Pontiac. His win-loss eliminations record for the season was an astounding 56-13, which was the best of his entire career, and twice he went on three-race winning streaks.

WJ missed a sweep of the strenuous Western Swing by one, falling in the final round to Jeg Coughlin in Denver. He then reached the winner's circle back to back at Sonoma and Seattle. Over the course of the season, he logged his 100th No. 1–qualifier award and 150th top speed, set low ET of the event at 13 of the 22 events on the tour, and claimed top speed of the meet 21 times.

"What a difference a year makes," said WJ from the podium as he accepted his fourth NHRA Pro Stock championship trophy at the NHRA Winston Championship Awards Ceremony. "I knew we had the nucleus of a winning team this season if we were willing to make the commitment and sacrifice."

WJ's Firebird bore Good-wrench Service Plus branding in 1998 and saw the inside of 9 winner's circles in 12 final rounds. An incredible 56-13 win-loss record was a ticket to the championship (WJ's fourth) and gave him the assurance that he needed to shift from refining the new Firebird back to his true passion: engine development. (Photo Courtesy Evan J. Smith)

WJ was reluctant to select a favorite car or a favorite race, but the GM Goodwrench Service Plus Pontiac Firebird with a special Superman paint scheme stands out. In 1999, he nabbed the pole at Indy and picked up his sixth U.S. Nationals win, but only through heroic efforts. After the first round of qualifying on Saturday, he flew back to the shop in Sugar Hill, Georgia, with a damaged cylinder head. After making the repairs to the damaged piece, he jetted back to Indianapolis and made it in time for Sunday eliminations. (Photo Courtesy Evan J. Smith)

WJ, near lane, and KJ are side by side in Sonoma in 1999. This photo was taken during Friday night qualifying. KJ was No. 1 with a 6.898-second pass at 199.91 mph, and his father was No. 2 on a 6.925 at a booming 200.77 mph. KJ won the event on Sunday by defeating Jim Yates in the final round. (Photo Courtesy Auto Imagery)

The Professor's Way: Lesson 19

"At that time [the 1990s], there was more availability of better materials," Warren Johnson said. "I don't think a lot of people investigated that as diligently as we did, and it helped our performance and reliability.

"The other thing was that I always looked at racing as a 24-hour-a-day job, and I never punched a time clock because I just worked until whatever particular operation I was working on was complete. Then I'd move on to the next one."

WJ acquired a new Rick Jones–built Pontiac for the 1999 season and spent ample time in the wind tunnel testing. He and his crew also designated significant man hours to searching for horsepower over the winter after two solid years devoted to chassis development.

Although research and development was constant, WJ revealed that he won the 1998 championship with an engine originally built in 1995. It had the same cam and cylinder heads on it that were used three years prior.

"We know we have a race car that can handle the horsepower, so now we can go back to working on the engines," he said.

The 1999 season proved that time was well-spent in both arenas. The first three races were all about family, as brothers Jeg and Troy Coughlin went head-to-head at the

The 30th anniversary Trans Am made its debut at the 1999 Winternationals. The white "Warbird" was a striking contrast to the black and silver Firebird that propelled him to nine victories in 1998, his fourth championship season. "I'm not superstitious about colors, but the last time I raced a white car was in 1993 when I won my second Pro Stock championship," said WJ ahead of the season. And sure enough, he locked down championship No. 5 in 1999.

The brand-new Pontiac Grand Am that would debut for the 2001 season is in the Lockheed Martin wind tunnel for testing. WJ was in a Pontiac Firebird from 1996 to 2000. The Grand Am proved immediately to be successful, as he drove it to his sixth and final NHRA Pro Stock world championship.

WJ won the sixth NHRA Pro Stock championship of his career in 2001, driving the Goodwrench Service Plus Pontiac Grand Am in its first season. That's Ron Krisher in the near lane. (Photo Courtesy Evan J. Smith)

The 2001 Pontiac Grand Am makes its debut at the season-opening NHRA Winternationals. WJ drove it to the semifinals in a strong opening act for the season. (Photo Courtesy Auto Imagery)

Winternationals (Jeg got the nod), KJ got the best of Troy in Phoenix, and then the Johnson family took over with another father-and-son final. WJ bested KJ in Gainesville, and then Mike Edwards took a 1-2 punch from the team in the next two finals: KJ won at Houston and WJ won the spring Dallas race.

WJ reached seven more finals that season, including a victory at the fall race in Dallas, where this time there were no mixed feelings. WJ secured the championship with a final-round defeat of Yates.

The Dallas event was a clean sweep, as WJ set both ends of the national record in qualifying with his 6.822-second pass at 202.33 mph. He logged his 15th No. 1 of the season, bringing his earnings for the year from the Holley Pro Stock low qualifier bonus program to $45,000.

Still as frugal as ever, WJ expressed his appreciation of the Holley bonus, saying, "These things run on money, not gasoline."

After KJ lost in the first round, WJ had the opportunity to clinch the championship, but he had to win the race to do so. In the final, he wheeled his GM Goodwrench Pontiac Firebird to a 6.842 at 201.74 mph and left Yates in his vapor trails. His opponent crossed the finish line just after with a 6.892 at 199.24 mph.

"The car was awesome on the final run," said WJ. "I stuck it in second gear, and it just hiked up the front end and marched right to the finish line. I'll enjoy the championship for about a half hour, and then I have to get back to work."

Back to work he went, and at the next race, the fall

At the podium at the 2001 NHRA Award Ceremony, KJ honored his father, who had claimed his sixth world championship. KJ came just short of winning a championship of his own over the course of his career and finished No. 2 in the nation four times with 40 national event wins.

Houston event, he reset the national record for speed again with a 202.36. He reached one more final round—at the NHRA Finals, where Jeg Coughlin triggered the win light.

WJ's sixth and final NHRA Pro Stock championship was earned in 2001 in the GM Goodwrench Service Plus Pontiac Grand Am. He was a perfect 6 for 6 in final rounds with three No. 1–qualifier awards.

WJ's accomplishments were particularly impressive in a season that saw 14 different winners in 23 races. WJ was one of just four drivers able to repeat that year, with Jeg Coughlin winning three to be second-best in final rounds. Coughlin, though, finished fifth in the nation behind Jim Yates, Bruce Allen, and Mike Edwards.

Brand Shift

At the end of 1995, Oldsmobile's marketing needs shifted as the company sought to promote the Aurora V-8, a 4-valve engine that didn't realistically fit an NHRA category, let alone the precise confines of Pro Stock. With Oldsmobile's redirection, WJ's contract was transferred intact to another GM brand: Pontiac.

"I never had any animosity with GM at all, never had any issues with the engineers or anything over there, but the change to Pontiac was a challenge for some of the fans," recalled WJ. "There were some people who voiced their opinion about it because they would rather see me in an Oldsmobile, but the truth is that I'd race an International pickup. I can't read the name on the hood when I'm going down the racetrack."

The organization had first signed on in 1986 with WJ's black and silver Oldsmobile Firenza with GM Goodwrench Performance Parts on the door. In 1988, WJ's new Oldsmobile was adorned with the red, white, and blue colors of ACDelco. GM Performance Parts returned as a major sponsor in his 1993 and 1995 championship seasons, and WJ debuted the fresh GM Goodwrench Service Plus colors with its backing in 1997.

WJ ended the decade on an upswing. On the heels of clinching his fifth world championship, he signed a three-year contract extension with GM Service Parts Operations to campaign its GM Goodwrench Service Plus brand through 2002.

During the 1990s, WJ won 30 percent of the races and appeared in 44 percent of the final rounds. He ended his reign over the decade in top form by setting top speed at every event on the NHRA's 1999 schedule. He was the first driver in NHRA history to record top speed of every event on the schedule in one season. (Photo Courtesy Auto Imagery)

CHAPTER 8

THE RIVALRIES

The concept of rivalries is at the very core of drag racing. Every race is man and machine versus man and machine. Unlike stick-and-ball sports, drag racing features one-on-one competition in which a single human is crowned champion of a respective category at the end of each season. It takes a number of individuals to put together a successful program, but at the end of the day, it all boils down to the capabilities of a single person harnessing the overwhelming horsepower of a single race car while the same situation is happening in the other lane. Drag racing is the breeding ground for deliciously contemptuous rivalries.

It sounds hateful, but the truth is that robust rivalries bring immense depth to competition, and that generates profound fan loyalty. Although drag racing is thrilling in its own right, at least if you're paying attention, the interest of observers intensifies greatly when they have skin in the game and respect a particular driver for one reason or another. Fans choose their favorite and are prone to get behind someone with whom they connect and/or admire. Brand loyalty in drag racing is a real thing, and many rivalries have been built upon that concept.

It began in his match racing days when Chevrolet pilot Warren Johnson and fellow Minnesotan John Hagen, a steadfast Mopar campaigner, inspired fans to choose and cheer for one or the other. Hagen and WJ, though, didn't have quite the same outward rivalry as some of his later competitors. As WJ's reputation and experience grew, more rivalries developed.

Johnson versus Shepherd

Lee Shepherd worked his way up from the Sportsman ranks with partners David Reher and Buddy Morrison. They were successful racing the NHRA's Modified class and ventured into the NHRA's Pro Stock class in 1976 with a Don Ness–built small-block Chevy Monza. A high-speed crash midseason halted the team's Pro Stock partnership temporarily, but they were back

Lee Shepherd's career was on an upward trajectory that was cut short when he died in 1985. From 1982 to 1984, Shepherd and his Reher-Morrison Chevrolet was WJ's lead competition when it came to horsepower and speed, at least in terms of the national records. Beginning at the 1982 Winternationals and until the testing incident in Ardmore, Oklahoma, that took his life in March 1985, Shepherd claimed six records for ET and two records for speed. Twice in that time period, WJ knocked Shepherd down a notch with speed records claimed in Indianapolis (179.28 mph) and Fremont (181.08), both in 1982. Here they are squaring off in the Brainerd final round at the 1984 Northstar Nationals. WJ won the match. (Photo Courtesy Auto Imagery)

Minnesota match racer John Hagen and his Barracuda were the other half of one of the very first rivalries in WJ's career. (Photo Courtesy John Foster Jr.)

The Professor's Way: Lesson 20

"I always approached it as a one-lane racetrack," Warren Johnson said. "I do the best I possibly can do in any particular situation for that one lane. If you get a bad lane, you have to figure out how the heck to get down it."

Bill "Grumpy" Jenkins and Bob Glidden at the NHRA Finals in 2001. Jenkins, a pioneer of the sport, laid the groundwork for Pro Stock that Glidden, Shepherd, Johnson, and so many more built upon. (Photo Courtesy Auto Imagery)

together again in 1978 with a Z28 Camaro powered by a small-block in place of the formerly favored V-8. Reher, Morrison, and Shepherd were serious contenders straightaway.

Shepherd had arrived on the Pro Stock scene just as WJ was pulling back to concentrate on the IHRA, where he won championships in 1979 and 1980. But before his

focus turned, a contentious spirit began to brew between the two—at least from Shepherd's perspective.

The division race at Bandimere Speedway near Denver was slated to take place in late June. The two-day race, with nearly 200 drivers entered across eight categories, was highly anticipated. The Denver-area fans were hungry to take in their first race of the year in 1978, when the division race preceded the national.

Heading into the event, WJ was a favorite. He had the longest winning streak in the history of NHRA division races with 13 consecutive victories in West Central meets. He had been unstoppable from the final Division 5 event in 1975 and through all of 1976 and 1977.

The division event in Pueblo, Colorado, earlier in the year saw Shepherd emerge as a threat. He was racing right alongside WJ throughout the weekend with a surge of power, but it was WJ in the final.

At the time, Shepherd held the national record for speed in NHRA Pro Stock (160.71 mph) and had called his shot. He told reporter Michael Knisley from the *Denver Post* for the June 1, 1978, issue that he would be heading to the Bandimere event solely to beat WJ.

Bob Glidden was leading the national points at the time, and Shepherd was No. 2, but he had his sights set on WJ after the narrow loss at Pueblo.

WJ told the *Denver Post*, "He doesn't affect me at all. People like that are racing for ego purposes, strictly. It doesn't matter to me at all what they think. I've got no rivalry with them."

Taking the relaxed disposition into eliminations, WJ calmly avoided any big throwdowns and won the race

The 1997 Dupont Automotive Finishes Pro Stock Challenge featured the top eight in the nation vying for bragging rights and $50,000. From left to right are Jim Yates, Troy Coughlin, WJ, KJ, Steve Schmidt, Mike Edwards, Jerry Eckman, and Pete Williams. "I never looked at any of the other competitors in a form of envy or intimidation," said WJ. "It never bothered me. I was single-focused on winning races. I never beat anybody, I was just able to win races." (Photo Courtesy Auto Imagery)

The classic rivalry of Warren Johnson versus Bob Glidden. This shot was captured at the NHRA finals at Orange County International Raceway in 1983. WJ won the event and defeated Lee Shepherd in the final. "Bob and I never discussed much of anything. When he won a race, I congratulated him, and he would do the same. There was no animosity there, and I guess that's because we both respected each other. We realized that between the two of us, we had the biggest percentage chance of winning any particular race." (Photo Courtesy Steve Reyes)

The Oldsmobile Calais that WJ wheeled in 1985 was good for two wins in five final rounds that year. Here he is racing Bob Glidden at the NHRA Winternationals in the final round. Glidden was the titlist at that event, but WJ evened the score at the very next race, the Gatornationals in Gainesville, where they again met in the final round. (Photo Courtesy Steve Reyes)

with low ET and top speed of the meet, a 9.32 at 144.46 mph, in his final run.

In 1981, WJ began his comeback while finishing out his tour with the IHRA. Shepherd was the champ that year, but in 1982, WJ turned up the heat.

Shepherd took an early lead and ran with it, reaching the first nine final rounds and winning six times. Midway through his assault on the class in 1982, WJ stepped into the picture and reached the final round in Montreal. It was the fourth final round of his career and the fourth runner-up, and WJ had just about enough. At the next event, the Summernationals in Englishtown, WJ beat Shepherd in the final round to claim his first NHRA national event win.

Although Shepherd was well ahead and clearly going to be the champion, WJ wasn't ready to hang up his sword for the season. He defeated the Texan at the last two races of the year in Fremont and Pomona.

Shepherd died in a testing accident in Oklahoma on March 11, 1985. In all, the two met in the final round at an NHRA national event seven times, and WJ won all but one.

Johnson versus Glidden

Bob Glidden, who mostly wheeled factory-backed Ford Pro Stockers throughout his career, was the driver that many consider WJ's biggest adversary. Glidden was a

Bob Glidden and WJ side by side at the U.S. Nationals. Glidden, an Indiana native, was quite successful on the venerable grounds of the Indianapolis-area drag strip with nine wins over the course of his career. WJ ruffled his feathers there a time or two and has six Indy wins of his own. This image was taken in 1992, a year that WJ claimed a U.S. Nationals trophy. It was Larry Morgan that he defeated in the final round though. (Photo Courtesy Steve Reyes)

WJ and Arlene pose for a photo in 1987 with family friend Anthony Caruso and Bob Glidden in Baton Rouge.

WJ's nephew, Ragen, with Bob Glidden. Although Glidden and WJ were very much "two dogs fighting over the same bone," as WJ has said, they didn't dislike one another. They just kept their heads down and kept to themselves, and the two never really spoke many words to one another.

regular record-breaker in NHRA competition from the early 1970s and on through the 1980s, a role that WJ took over in his powerful domination of the 1990s.

WJ first ran into Glidden in Rockford, Illinois, at a match race. Immediately, he identified that Glidden was a tenacious racer doing the best he possibly could. It was a bit like looking in the mirror.

"You have to really have a passion for this sport in order to be successful," said WJ to Lewis Bloom for an *NHRA Today* interview in 2017, shortly after Glidden died at the age of 73.

"He would do whatever it took to win a race," WJ said. "It was pretty crude work once in a while, but the ultimate result was that he got the job done. I think he gave inspiration to a lot of people and showed them that if you dedicate yourself to something, the amount of work that you put into it will dictate your success."

Glidden earned a total of 10 championships and 85 national event wins over the course of his career. Throughout the 1980s, WJ and Glidden often finished side by side in the Pro Stock points. In 1982, they were No. 3 and No. 4, with WJ on top. They switched places in 1983, when Glidden finished third and Johnson fourth.

The 1984 season brought about their first two final-round showdowns, and WJ won them both with trophies in Montreal and then at Indianapolis, Glidden's hometown race and what many considered his sacred territory. The two finished the season No. 2 (WJ) and No. 3 (Glidden).

Glidden was the champion in 1985, 1986, and 1988, with WJ trailing just behind in the No. 2 position. During that period, they raced one another for the trophy 10 times. WJ won their last final-round battle at the Seattle event in 1995. In all, the two squared off in 18 final rounds during the course of their time in NHRA together with Glidden holding a 12-6 advantage.

"Back then, you could make money at it. Glidden and I were both

WJ's nephew Ragen with Rusty Glidden at Brainerd in 1986. Ragen enjoyed coming to the races when they made it back to Minnesota to tag along with WJ. He was a fan of Glidden, as well.

A (Mostly) Friendly Family Feud

The Johnson and Glidden families stood out among their competitors because they didn't have hired crew, instead the family was the crew in each camp. WJ, his wife, Arlene, and son, KJ, were on one side of the Pro Stock pits while Glidden, his wife, Etta, and sons Billy and Rusty were on the other. Both teams were there to make a living rather than race as a hobby, and their livelihood depended on their success.

Broadcaster Steve Evans bravely stepped between the families to interview the women before the final round at the 1988 U.S. Nationals in Indianapolis, and he inquired as to the extent of the rivalry.

"It's a rivalry when we're on the starting line, but when it's all over, we're still friends," said Arlene with a broad smile.

Etta answered, grinning as well, "This is a very competitive sport. I wish them well, but I wish us better."

Glidden and WJ were equally matched heading into the final, both putting a 7.37 on the scoreboard in the semifinals. WJ left the starting line too early and illuminated the red light in the money round, and Glidden got the win on a 7.34.

Darrell Alderman and WJ in 1992. The two met one another 11 times in the final round, with WJ holding a 6-5 advantage when all was said and done. (Photo Courtesy Steve Reyes)

Tony Christian (near lane) competed in Modified Production before moving into the Pro Stock category. WJ raced him once in a Pro Stock final round (in Atlanta in 1988) and was the victor. Christian claimed his first win in the class over Kenny Delco at the next race on tour, the Mid-South Nationals in Memphis. Christian went on to defeat Bob Glidden in Brainerd later that year and then Darrell Alderman at the Chief Nationals in Dallas in 1990.

just trying to make a living racing," said WJ. He explained that between the purse and what the contingency program paid, a racer could make around $40,000 a weekend at that time.

"It wasn't that we disliked one another, we were just fiercely competitive because we were two dogs fighting for the same bone. I don't think we spoke 10 words in 20 years."

On July 22, 2001, then 58-year-old WJ earned the 86th Pro Stock trophy of his career at Denver's Mile-High Nationals. With the win, he moved ahead of Glidden as the most prolific driver in NHRA Pro Stock history and became the second-most-winning driver in all professional categories (Funny Car racer John Force was at the head of the class).

Johnson versus the Dodge Boys

The most controversial of WJ's competitors were Mopar wheelmen Darrell Alderman and Scott Geoffrion, teammates best known as Wayne County Speed Shop's Dodge Boys.

The Dodge Boys were branded as youthful and contemporary, relatively clean-cut, and completely all-American. They were great drivers, but beneath the surface, as is often true for actual human beings, they might not have been quite as squeaky clean as they appeared.

Alderman, after winning the championship in 1990 and 1991, was suspended from NHRA competition due to a legal issue outside of racing. Geoffrion, who had been the research and development driver for WJ during that time, was asked by Mopar if he would fill the seat in Alderman's absence heading into the 1992 season. WJ supported the move for a man he considered to be his friend, but when Alderman returned in 1994 to form a two-car team with Geoffrion, tension quickly escalated.

WJ and Alderman first met in a final round in 1991, and they had plenty of opportunities to trade wins that season. Alderman got the nod in their first two meetings (back to back in Pomona and Phoenix), and then WJ was the winner in Gainesville and Memphis. In all, the two met seven times that year with Alderman holding a 4-3 advantage in final rounds over WJ by the time he had his hands around the championship trophy.

The 1992 season gave Geoffrion the opportunity to prove that the Professor had taught him well, and he met (and fell to) WJ twice that year in final rounds. Geoffrion again held down the fort for Dodge in 1993 and again

> ### The Professor's Way: Lesson 21
>
> "I'd rather have the competition not notice me," Warren Johnson said. "It isn't like I wanted to sneak up on them, I just wanted to go about my business. It was never an ego thing for me. I'm too frugal to have that big an ego."

came up against WJ in two final rounds, both of which ended in the exact same manner as they had before.

NHRA's 1994 Pro Stock Scorecard	
Location	**Result**
Pomona, California 1	WJ def. Darrell Alderman
Phoenix, Arizona	Scott Geoffrion def. Alderman
Houston, Texas	WJ def. Geoffrion
Gainesville, Florida	WJ def. Alderman
Atlanta, Georgia	Geoffrion def. WJ
Memphis, Tennessee	Alderman def. Geoffrion
Englishtown, New Jersey	Larry Morgan def. Alderman
Columbus, Ohio	Geoffrion def. Jim Yates
Topeka, Kansas 1	Geoffrion def. Yates
Denver, Colorado	Alderman def. Mark Osborne
Sonoma, California	Alderman def. Geoffrion
Seattle, Washington	Steve Schmidt def. Yates
Brainerd, Minnesota	Yates def. Osborne
Indianapolis, Indiana	WJ def. Mark Pawuk
Reading, Pennsylvania	Alderman def. WJ
Topeka, Kansas 2	Geoffrion def. Alderman
Dallas, Texas	Geoffrion def. WJ
Pomona, California 2	Alderman def. Geoffrion

Alderman returned for the 1994 season, and he and Geoffrion became a formidable 1-2 punch that rocked the Pro Stock world. No one was more rocked, however, than WJ. Alderman and Geoffrion regularly lined up on opposite sides of the ladder on Sunday, setting up a total of four all-Mopar final rounds and putting either one or both of the Dodge Pro Stockers in the final round at all but three races out of the 18 contested that year.

WJ reached the final six times, more than any driver outside of the Dodge Boys, and battled tooth and nail for four wins. Only once did he face a challenger outside of the Mopar lot: he claimed victory over Mark Pawuk at the U.S. Nationals.

Alderman's 5 wins in 10 trophy rounds, plus nine No. 1 qualifiers, translated to his third and final championship. Geoffrion won 6 times in 10 finals and was No. 1 qualifier twice, which was good for second place. WJ,

Scott Geoffrion was a teammate before he was a rival. In 1991, he drove the second ACDelco Olds for the team and became quite close with the Johnson family. He and KJ were very good friends even after he began racing with a competing team. (Photo Courtesy Les Welch Family)

with 6 low qualifier awards and his 4 wins in 6 finals, finished No. 3 in the world.

National records, also worth valuable points, were recorded by Geoffrion in Houston (196.59 mph), WJ in Atlanta (197.15), KJ in Englishtown (6.988, the first sub-7-second pass), and Alderman in Sonoma (197.80).

"It was a little bump in the road, but that bump only lasted a few years," said WJ. "There was a more intense rivalry between Glidden and myself than I had with the Dodges."

At the height of their adversarial relationship, many in the community believed that the Dodge Boys were up to no good. Allegations of illegal power enhancements were never proven though, and when the Wayne County Speed Shop was reportedly broken into and all of their engines were destroyed, they were knocked to their knees midway through the 1995 season and were never quite able to rebound.

WJ initially shrugged off the frustration in a 2015 interview with WFO Radio's Joe Castello, saying "We knew what was going on there, it was just a matter of proving it."

When pressed further about the fact that some say the Dodge Boys stole the championship from the Professor, he 'fessed up to a few hard feelings.

"The part that was most annoying to me was what their shenanigans cost me financially," he said. "I liked Scott, and Darrell and I got along just great off the track. But at the racetrack, it was all business. Actually, had they

Scott Geoffrion, after he drove for WJ and moved on to Team Mopar, is in the staging lanes with WJ's crew chief Greg Anderson. Dicken Wear, CEO of "The Original Competition Engineering since 1954" and editor in chief of The Motorsports Report, once asked WJ what he thought about some of the racers who used to work for him and were now racing against him. WJ replied, "I taught them everything they know; I didn't teach them everything I know."

One Year Later

National Dragster Editor Phil Burgess described the 1994 Houston burndown between Geoffrion and WJ in great detail in 2009. He also told an entertaining story about what happened the following year in Houston when WJ and Geoffrion were paired together in qualifying.

"As they prepared to stage, a trio of dogs jumped the guard wall on the top end, and WJ and Geoffrion were shut off on the starting line. Never one to miss an opportunity to needle, WJ later quipped, 'I didn't know what was going on until someone on the starting-line crew told me there were dogs on the track. My response was, I know, he's in the other lane.'"

not been there, Pro Stock racing might not have been as exciting. Even though I didn't particularly enjoy that whole period of time, it probably did drag racing some good. I looked at the sport overall, not just for my own personal gain. If the sport didn't survive, neither would I. It was one of those things. You just grin and bear it."

Geoffrion was a friend to the Johnson family well before he was a teammate and long before he was a rival. In 1991, WJ asked Geoffrion if he would like to drive a second car for the team to help with some research and development. It was the dawn of the two-car team concept, and WJ, always thinking, knew that if he could have two cars out there gathering data, he could make tremendous strides in half the time. Geoffrion readily accepted and proved to be a quick study.

The two met up that year for the first time in a challenge for the trophy, and WJ came away with that Denver win.

In Geoffrion's 1991 turn behind a second Oldsmobile for WJ, he competed in 18 races, scored 2 runner-up finishes, 2 No. 1–qualifying positions, and ended the year No. 4 in the championship standings.

In 1992, when Geoffrion moved over to the Mopar team, they met again in the final on two occasions. Both times it was WJ who waltzed off with the trophy. WJ claimed two more victories over Geoffrion in 1993, and by that time, Geoffrion was likely wondering if he'd ever get past the Professor.

Their sixth money-round match started on quite a different note than any of their previous battles. The 1994 season began with a win for WJ over Alderman in Pomona, and then Geoffrion scored the Phoenix trophy over his Dodge teammate. The next race was Houston, where Geoffrion was the No. 1 qualifier with a 7.03, Alderman was No. 2 on a 7.061, and WJ was No. 3 by way of a 7.065.

Geoffrion worked through his side of the ladder on Sunday, taking out Jerry Eckman and Mark Pawuk before laying down his best time of the day, a 7.07, to defeat KJ and score a ticket to the final. WJ socked away wins over Steve Schmidt and Jim Yates to set up a big battle

with Alderman in the semis, where his own 7.07 was just enough for lane choice over Geoffrion.

The crowd was wide awake as the two rivals made their burnouts. They really began to roar after Geoffrion and WJ activated their pre-stage bulbs and then simply sat motionless, idling for nearly a minute, neither intending to stage first.

NHRA Chief Starter Buster Couch was having none of it. He motioned angrily that both drivers should stage, but neither would budge. A handful of seconds after their obstinate denial to comply, a frustrated Couch decided time was up. He waved them out of the beams and instructed them to shut off their engines. After a brief cooldown period, he told them to fire back up and stage within 10 seconds.

This time, Geoffrion and WJ did as they were told. WJ went in first, quickly followed by his opponent. They left the starting line just 0.017 second apart, Geoffrion with the slight edge, but it was WJ at the finish-line stripe, 7.07 to 7.10.

At the top end, adrenaline was surging.

"The kid's just a jerk out there," WJ responded to the television anchor's inquisition just as he was emerging from the winning car. "I was just trying to play his game. He better learn how to drive a race car before he tries playing games like that."

The reporter, stoking the fire, said, "But it looked like both of you were playing the game. Anybody can stage at any time."

"I don't have to stage last or first. I'll stage when I'm ready," said WJ, who looked over his shoulder at Geoffrion, who had just gotten out of his car. "You wanna play that game again, Scott?"

"Hey, I'll play any game you want," replied Geoffrion. "Trust me. Hey, put the gloves on right now."

Greg Anderson, then crew chief for WJ, years later recalled the situation as slightly comical.

"I was laughing to myself up there on the starting line," said Anderson. "Buster Couch was something else—if you got in that man's face, he'd knock you down. He did not put up with any BS, but those two didn't care.

They were running their own race, and they didn't want to stage. It seemed like half an hour. Warren got it done and taught Scott a little bit of a lesson in the process. It was kind of cool from my end."

WJ later stated that everybody knew Geoffrion was told to stage last by team manager Dave Hutchens. WJ said he was willing to wait for his Social Security check if that was what it took.

Despite the intense on-track opposition, the tension off-track was minimal and faded away completely over the years. When Geoffrion died of an apparent heart attack on May 8, 2006, at the age of 40, it was felt deeply by WJ.

"Scott was one of those special people who didn't have an enemy in the world," he said. "He was a good racer and just a great person to have around. Even though we would go on to have our well-publicized staging battles, we never stopped being friends. He was a genuinely nice guy who was taken away from us much too soon."

Geoffrion, in an interview with NHRA three years before his untimely passing, expressed gratitude for the time he spent with WJ.

"Even if you're not the sharpest knife in the drawer, you're going to learn something by just being around Warren," he said. "He is the smartest guy out here in drag racing. . . . He's never going to teach you everything he knows, but you certainly will learn a lot."

I Spy

Quiet, methodical, and intensely focused, WJ came off as more than a little unapproachable to fellow racers. What gave him such an advantage in terms of power and speed was a mystery in a class built around proprietary secrets and the shielding of parts and pieces potentially capable of coercing gains. WJ's success was a mystery the competition desperately wanted to solve.

At one point, a well-known racer and his engine builder were caught lying under the trailer attempting to

Greg Anderson and WJ's crew review the time slip after the Atlanta final round. The margin of victory for WJ was a wee 0.004 second. (Photo Courtesy Auto Imagery)

Greg Anderson and WJ raced for the trophy in the 2003 final round at Atlanta. It was their first final round since 1999, when WJ had defeated his former protégé in the Indy money round. In Atlanta, it was WJ again with the win after he clocked a 0.018-second reaction time and paired it with a 6.853 at 201.46 to knock out his challenger on a holeshot. Anderson was 0.036 at the tree and 6.839, 202.94 at the finish-line stripe. (Photo Courtesy Auto Imagery)

photograph WJ's headers. On another occasion, a prominent Pro Stock team hired a photographer to shoot down from the grandstands and into Johnson's pit area so that they could determine what kind of manifold he was using. It was a sheet metal–fabricated intake manifold at the time when everyone else was using cast intake manifolds, but that was not revealed because every photo came out blurry. Unbeknownst to the offending team, WJ had gone to school with the photographer, who clued him in.

"It was just part of the game," explained WJ. "Espionage was just part of their efforts to be more competitive. Some people think R&D means rip off and duplicate."

Johnson versus Anderson

KJ Johnson and Greg Anderson were both born and raised in Minnesota with fathers who possessed a passion for the auto industry. Rod Anderson, Greg's father, owned a car dealership and did some racing of his own at the Sportsman level, taking his son along for the ride. The younger Anderson eventually earned a job on the crew for Minnesota racer John Hagen, and through that connection, he met the Johnson family.

KJ and Greg were in their 20s at the time, just a couple of years apart in age, and they would cross paths here and there at racetracks in the area. After Hagen was killed in a very bad crash at Brainerd International Raceway on August 19, 1983, Greg stepped away from the racing scene. KJ was the one who brought him back.

"Two or three years had passed, and we needed help, so I just called him," said KJ. "He was good help. We would drive down the road with the truck and trailer, and we had fun."

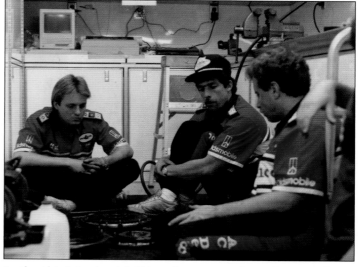

In the think tank with KJ and crewmembers Greg Anderson and John Caruso.

KJ and Greg formed a strong friendship as they worked side by side during several of Johnson's championship seasons and during the challenging years with the Dodge Boys. They were experiencing racing in all of its finest and harshest moments, and both were learning the intricacies of the ultracompetitive Pro Stock category along the way.

"When Greg came to work for us, he didn't know a piston from a petunia," laughed WJ. "I had to show him how to set up ring gears and everything. He was a fast learner, though, and I give him credit for that. He had a good work ethic."

Realizing that he could better communicate with his crew if they understood the inner workings of the car from every angle, WJ enrolled KJ and Anderson in Roy Hill's Drag Racing School and, of course, footed the bill.

"They were there damn near a week," he said, somewhat perturbed at the memory. "It was a week of two people out of the shop not doing anything, but we had to all get on the same page if we were going to move forward. When I would tell them something, I needed them to be able to download and process that information."

The idea worked, but it was accompanied by an unexpected side effect. Both young men came to understand what it felt like to drive a Pro Stock car and, thus, both developed the urge to drive one of their own. Once the wheels were

While most of their time was spent at the racetrack, Arlene made it a point to schedule special stops on occasion. In 1987, they visited wineries after the Sonoma event in Northern California. Pictured here from left to right are Greg Anderson, Kathy Ketron, Arlene, WJ, and KJ.

in motion, it was just a matter of time. KJ's time came sooner than Anderson's when he made his Pro Stock debut in 1993, but they would both become noted and celebrated drivers on their own respective merit in the years that followed.

Anderson approached WJ in 1997, 11 years after coming on board with the team, and asked what WJ thought about Anderson leaving to drive a Pro Stock car for Troy Humphrey, his future father-in-law.

WJ was agreeable, but it took about a year before Anderson actually made the jump. Finally, in 1998, the man who would become one of the Professor's most noted protégés made his debut in Humphrey's Pontiac Firebird in Columbus.

"I told him that if he hesitated and didn't take the opportunity, he would wonder about it the rest of his life,"

Greg Anderson accepted Crew Chief of the Year honors in 1992 following WJ's first NHRA championship season. WJ claimed four low-qualifier awards that year and reset the national record for speed three times. He was the only driver in the class to touch the speed record that season, which topped out at 194.51 mph. (Photo Courtesy Auto Imagery)

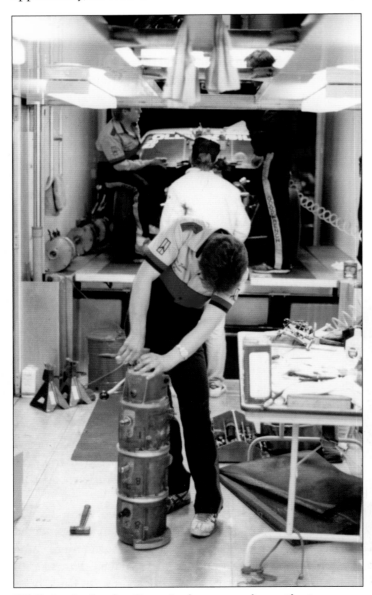

While in the hauler, Greg Anderson works on the transmission as part of the Warren Johnson Racing crew in 1987.

A very young Greg Anderson in the pit area. The Minnesota native was sent to Roy Hill's Drag Racing School by WJ and got the taste for driving. "I felt then, and still feel, that you have to get to the same level of education and experience to have effective communication," said WJ of his decision to send KJ and Anderson to Hill's school. "When you have three minds working together on the same project, and you're all on the same level, the possibility of achieving a good result is infinitely better. Sending them to Roy's school was probably one of the best things I did. Overall, it worked out for all of us, really."

said WJ. "It's better to fail at something you want to try than to never try it. You learn from your failures. Or at least, you should."

Anderson didn't make the field in Columbus, but he came back for the following race in St. Louis and qualified in the No. 16 spot, which set up a first-round meeting with No. 1 qualifier WJ on Sunday.

WJ's rookie opponent was a touch quicker as the two left the starting line: Anderson with a 0.465-second reaction time (back then, 0.400 was a perfect light) to a 0.487, and the two tripped the 60-foot timers with identical numbers (a 1.061 for each). But Anderson got loose near the eighth-mile cones, and veteran racer WJ scored a relatively easy win: 7.012 seconds at 197.06 mph to 7.091 seconds at 194.25 mph.

The two lined up next to one another in elimination rounds many times over the years, including in the second round of what likely stands to be WJ's final NHRA race, the 2014 Southern Nationals at Atlanta.

In their final head-to-head match, Anderson was

The Professor's Way: Lesson 22

"If you concern yourself about who is in the other lane, that means you're taking it personally," Warren Johnson said. "You're trying to beat them. I never cared who was in the other lane; I just wanted to win the race. To me, that was success. That's why we're here."

well aware of the fact that one should never take the Professor lightly, and he left the starting line first with a 0.012-second reaction to WJ's respectable 0.034. WJ got loose as his Pontiac neared the finish line and had to click it off, sending Anderson ahead on a 6.561, 211.89 to 6.771, 179.92.

Generally, when the story of Anderson's career is told, one of the first things mentioned is that he was WJ's crew chief. Indeed, Anderson was an integral part of the team during several of the WJ's championship seasons.

"It was a pretty amicable parting of ways," said WJ. "I've always approached it as, the people who work for

The Phoenix final in 2006 pitted WJ against his former crew chief, Greg Anderson. It had been two years since their most recent final-round standoff, and this time it was WJ with a 0.015-second reaction time and clean 6.770-second pass at 206.13 to take the win. Anderson had trouble from the start in his lane and could only watch as the Professor raced ahead. The trophy was the 96th for WJ and his third at the Phoenix facility. (Photo Courtesy Auto Imagery)

There were many hugs for Arlene on the starting line after his defeat of Anderson. (Photo Courtesy Auto Imagery)

The Phoenix victory was the lone trophy for WJ in 2006, and he was back in the winner's circle four years later with his St. Louis win. "Outthinking the competition is what keeps me going," said WJ in 2000. (Photo Courtesy Auto Imagery)

me, I just hope I have a positive impact on the rest of their life. I would think that they probably learned more here than anyplace else they've been employed. If Greg could utilize what he learned for his own benefit, that's fine with me."

Anderson appeared to have learned much from his 10 years working with WJ. After racing with father-in-law Troy Humphrey, Anderson started a team of his own with Las Vegas businessman and racing devotee Ken Black in 2003. By the end of the 2019 season, he had accumulated 4 Pro Stock championships and 94 national event wins—just 3 fewer than Johnson's 97, which were then the most in the class and second-most in any professional NHRA category.

The Professor was in no way perturbed when asked about his thoughts on losing his standing as the most-winning driver in the class.

WJ defeated Greg Anderson to earn the trophy at the U.S. Nationals in 1999. "Some people like racing one particular racer because they find it to be a motivational situation," said WJ. "I never looked at it that way. There wasn't a person that particularly motivated me because I'm self-motivated. I don't care what it is that I'm doing, I want to be successful—that's what motivates me. I guess I'm just wired that way."

Warren Johnson's Complete List of NHRA Final-Round Opponents	
Opponent	Record
1. Larry Lombardo	0-1
2. Wally Booth	0-2
3. Lee Shepherd	6-1
4. Bob Glidden	6-12
5. Bruce Allen	3-2
6. Butch Leal	2-1
7. Don Coonce	1-0
8. Tony Christian	1-0
9. Morris Johnson Jr.	1-0
10. Larry Morgan	5-3
11. Darrell Alderman	6-5
12. Scott Geoffrion	7-2
13. Mark Pawuk	4-0
14. Jerry Eckman	3-0
15. Rickie Smith	2-0
16. Don Beverley	0-1
17. Kurt Johnson	10-3
18. Jim Yates	11-5
19. Steve Schmidt	2-1
20. Lewis Worden	1-0

Warren Johnson's Complete List of NHRA Final-Round Opponents	
Opponent	Record
21. Mike Edwards	3-1
22. Chuck Harris	0-1
23. Mike Thomas	1-1
24. Tom Martino	1-0
25. Jeg Coughlin	4-6
26. V. Gaines	1-1
27. Richie Stevens Jr.	2-0
28. Troy Coughlin	3-0
29. Greg Anderson	3-2
30. Brad Jeter	2-0
31. Mark Osborne	1-0
32. Ron Krisher	1-0
33. Allen Johnson	1-0
34. Dave Connolly	1-1
35. Jason Line	1-1
This list is in order of first final-round meeting.	

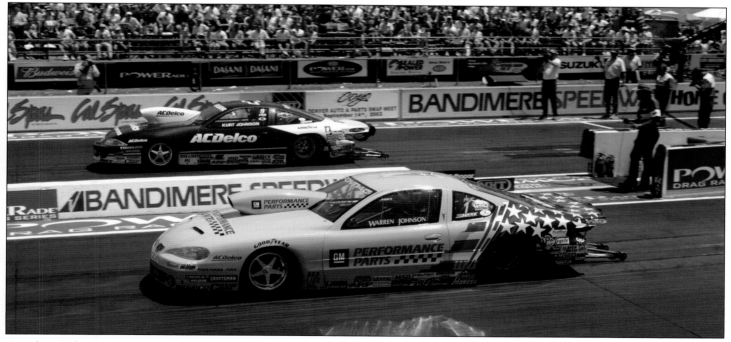

Another Johnson-versus-Johnson elimination round. This one took place in Denver at Bandimere Speedway, where KJ got a bit of a jump on the starting line, but dear ole Dad moved swiftly past with low ET of the round, a 7.285 at 189.44 mph to his son's 7.444 at 187.89 mph, to advance to the semifinals. "I think the biggest difference between us and other two-car teams is that we looked at it as a business," said WJ. "If we had a win and a runner-up and qualified No. 1, that meant we swept the table. For most people, this is an ego-driven thing. But we never looked at it that way." (Photo Courtesy Auto Imagery)

CHAPTER 9

THE PROFESSOR'S STUDENT

The Phoenix race in 2004 set up a second-round father-and-son meeting. Heading into the round, WJ was 36-15 in elimination wins over KJ and had most recently sent his son away empty handed in the semifinals at the season-opener the weekend before. This time, it was KJ's turn for a win light as he launched off the starting line first and made haste to the finish-line stripe, where he claimed a 6.834 at 203.31 mph over a 6.861 at 202.58 mph. KJ went on to win the race over Dave Connolly. (Photo Courtesy Auto Imagery)

"One of the biggest testaments to WJ's success is Kurt," said *National Dragster* Editor Phil Burgess. "I know his own driving ability had a lot to do with it, but Kurt has had a pretty impressive career. I attribute that to WJ horsepower, WJ preparation, and what he taught his son."

It seems absurd to think that the Professor of Pro Stock could possibly produce offspring that had no interest in driving a race car, but that's what WJ recalls from the first three decades of his only son's life. In fact, when KJ was a teen, he wanted to be an ophthalmologist for a short while.

"He never expressed an interest in racing. He might have wished for it, but he never verbally expressed it," said WJ, who is the first person to tell you he is not a mind reader.

The two simply never discussed it, and there would be no ignition without a discussion. KJ admits that it had been on his mind for some time before he spoke his wishes out loud.

"I probably always wanted to drive," KJ said. "I had a go-kart, motorbikes, stuff like that. It was a matter of the education of driving, more than anything. I knew I could do it, I just had to go out there, make laps, and really prove it to myself. I probably didn't express it early enough, that I wanted to drive, but we didn't have the financial backing anyway."

WJ and his small crew were at a Goodyear Tire test in Florida the first time KJ told him that he wanted to let the clutch out and see what it felt like. WJ had zero qualms about it and told his son, "Go ahead; there's the car."

KJ's impromptu education as he sat in the cockpit of the Oldsmobile Calais included a simple explanation of procedure and the admonition that if he was uncomfortable at any point, he should not proceed.

"The first time he got in the car, he let the clutch out and shut it off before it even went in second gear," said WJ with a big grin. "I asked him, 'Did it break?' He told me he let the clutch out and all he saw was blue sky. He wasn't expecting the acceleration to slam him back in the seat that hard, so he wisely shut it off. To me, it was kind of funny. But he did two or three more of those, and then he went to second gear, then third, and so on."

WJ and son, KJ, race in the Denver final in 2001. WJ was first to leave the starting line and first to the finish: 7.283 at 189.71 mph to 7.285 at 189.15 mph. Their money-round match was the 13th time that the two had squared off in a father-son final round. Their first dated back to 1993 in Atlanta, which was the first in the history of the sport in any professional class. (Photo Courtesy Auto Imagery)

KJ as a baby. He's already wrenching away.

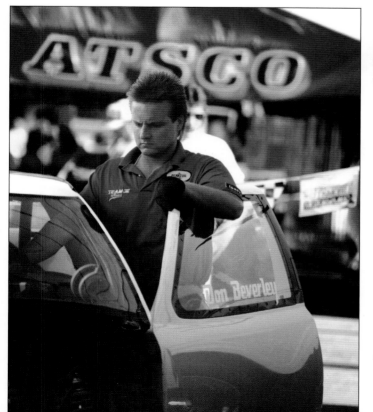

KJ had a front-row seat for his father's climb to the top in what could arguably be christened the most technologically advanced category in drag racing, NHRA Pro Stock. He observed his father work relentlessly toward the goal of supporting his family through his racing endeavors and applied what he knew to his own program. Some called him a natural talent, but KJ admits that there was a learning curve that included three crashes very early in his career. He learned from each error, though, and put together an honorable scorecard of 40 wins in 79 final rounds with 29 No. 1-qualifier awards. He competed in 454 national events between his debut in 1993 and the Atlanta race in 2014.

WJ's partnership with GM/Oldsmobile grew through the years as he established himself as a man who can think his way through any problem. Son KJ, shown working inside one of the new chassis, followed in his father's footsteps and, as WJ said, is very good at seeing a problem and determining the solution.

Greg Anderson and KJ are in the midst of an engine change at Brainerd's Northstar Nationals in 1987. They made up the crew for WJ in the late 1980s through much of the 1990s.

It was another seven years before WJ sent KJ and crewman Greg Anderson to Roy Hill's Drag Racing School, but the seed was planted.

The Rookie

Midway through 1992, between the Sonoma and Seattle races, the Johnson team took a detour to Woodburn, Oregon, for a little bonus track time. KJ had already been through Roy Hill's Drag Racing School and spent some time in the Pro Stock car in a handful of testing-type situations, but WJ felt that his son would benefit from some seat time in a competitive environment. Gordie Rivera graciously allowed Kurt to drive his car at Woodburn Dragstrip, and the hook was lodged.

KJ in the staging lanes in 1990, three years before he settled into the driver's seat of his own Pro Stocker.

The young gun in his first Pro Stock car, one of his dad's former Oldsmobile Cutlass models. This photo was taken at Maple Grove Raceway in Reading, Pennsylvania, where three of KJ's 40 wins were delivered (1993, 1998, 2000). (Photo Courtesy Evan J. Smith)

Just prior to the 1993 NHRA season kickoff, the Pro Stock teams rallied at Houston Raceway Park for their annual test session and intramural event. While he was there, KJ ran the team's second car. He made a 7.09-second pass, matching the then-quickest official run in history. He was eager for more, but KJ didn't have official plans to debut at the Winternationals. Somehow, though, the stars aligned, and he was able to borrow a car from Jerry Haas.

In the first race of his NHRA career, KJ made the field and logged a semifinals finish. He wasn't making any friends along the way by defeating Team II driver Don Beverley in the first round. Beverley's Olds was quicker, but his crew chief in the other lane left the starting line first, and that was the decider when their respective packages were tallied. KJ went on to log a round win over Bob Glidden before he was stopped by his old pal, Scott Geoffrion.

WJ won the event, but KJ was third in the points leaving Pomona. With such a splendid start, the second-generation drag racer's perspective had shifted, so he borrowed a car from friend and fellow competitor Harry Scribner to race in Phoenix.

"We put our engine in there, and I qualified pretty well," said KJ. "But I couldn't see the tree in the right lane. So, we pushed the car up there Sunday morning, and I cut a hole in the window net to give me a better view. I won the first round, then second round I had to

run Scott again. I was in the right lane, the good lane, and when I let the clutch out, I could see he was out on me. I watched him the whole way down the track."

The rookie driver's disappointment was tremendously compounded as he approached the finish line stripe. Scribner's was the third car he'd driven in as many weeks, and the brake ratio he was dealing with was vastly different than the first two. KJ recalled that the Don Ness car he piloted in Houston had a ratio of 7:1, the Jerry

Forward-thinking fans appear delighted to get KJ's autograph before he made it big as a driver.

The Professor's Way: Lesson 23

"Kurt could prepare his car any way he wanted to," Warren Johnson said. "I gave him, pretty much, free rein. He'd look at the way mine was set up, but he was a little bit more of a free spirit, so he would test stuff I never had the time to test. That was an advantage to me in the long run."

A long, smoky burnout ahead of a pass for KJ in 1995. The second-generation racer hadn't yet locked into his first major sponsor. "It's much better than just standing there watching the car," said KJ after moving from the crew chief role to driver. "Before, you could make a change and watch the car and see what it did, now I can feel it." (Photo Courtesy Les Welch Family)

The second-generation driver won at least one race every year from 1995 until 2008, when he scored three wins in six final rounds. He was No. 2 in the national Pro Stock standings four times: 1993, 2000, 2003, and 2005. (Photo Courtesy Auto Imagery)

Assistant Crew Chief Danny Lappi stands watch over KJ launching from the starting line in 1995. (Photo Courtesy Les Welch Family)

Haas car in Pomona was 3:1, and the Scribner car's brake ratio was 15:1.

"I couldn't get the 'chute out, so I tapped the brakes and was gone," he said. The Pro Stocker was immediately out of control at high speed, veering violently to the right, skidding through the desert sand, and then sliding backward through a large puddle, which caused it to slam into a retaining wall. The impact with the wall forced the car to bounce back on four wheels, and it came to a stop destroyed.

"I got out of the car all pissed off at the finish line. I was mad I was late on the 'chute and that I just got beat," said KJ. "And then I found out he had red-lighted. It went from bad to worse."

It didn't take KJ long to win his first race. He was runner-up in Atlanta, Englishtown, and Columbus to his father, but in Seattle, he finally sealed the deal with a final-round defeat of Mark Pawuk. WJ and Arlene were right there celebrating with their son in the winner's circle in 1993.

Every bit his father's son, KJ had no intention of slowing down. He borrowed a car from Billy Ewing to race in Houston to continue the points chase. On the other side of camp, his father was rising in the points with a win at the Gatornationals over Larry Morgan.

Then came the historic final at Atlanta Dragway, the first-ever NHRA father-against-son final. It was the first of six times that the father and son would square off for the trophy that year. It was also the first of four times

After hours and when the work was done for the day, the good times were rolling in the race trailer. From left to right: Willy Evans, KJ, Bruce Dailey, and Arlene.

KJ earned Rookie of the Year honors and WJ locked down his second consecutive NHRA Pro Stock championship in 1993. (Photo Courtesy Auto Imagery)

that WJ would be the one to send his son home without a win in 1993.

KJ picked up his first trophy that year in Seattle over Mark Pawuk. He scored two more—at Reading and Dallas, both over his father—to finish No. 2 in the points and claim the title of the NHRA's Rookie of the Year. The rising star's first season was tumultuous. He drove seven different cars over the course of the season and crashed twice (Phoenix and Topeka), but he never lifted in his drive to chase the championship right alongside his father.

Kurt Johnson's Career Highlights	
Year	**Highlight**
1993	NHRA Rookie of the Year
1993, 2000, 2003, and 2005	NHRA championship runner-up
1994	First NHRA Pro Stock driver to make a run quicker than 7 seconds (6.988 seconds, May 20, 1994, at Englishtown); first member of Holley 6-Second Pro Stock Club
1995	Qualified for every race for the third consecutive season
1998	Third member of Speed-Pro 200-mph Pro Stock Club (200.13 mph, March 14, 1998, at Gainesville)
2000	Was perfect in final rounds, winning six times in six attempts
2001	Runner-up to WJ at Denver, where WJ surpassed Bob Glidden as Pro Stock's all-time victory leader
2003	Earned at least one No. 1–qualifier award for ninth consecutive season; won career-best 49 elimination rounds and went entire season without a first-round loss
2008	Extended streak of winning one race per season to 14; earned 500th career round-win
2009	Finished in Pro Stock top 10 for 17th consecutive season
2014	Competed in 454th Pro Stock event (Atlanta)

Car Control

After crashing in Phoenix in just his second race as a Pro Stock driver, KJ was undeterred. He got right back on the horse to continue what was developing into a very intense education.

At a midweek event in Nobile, Oklahoma, just a short time later, KJ continued his hands-on education by effectively maneuvering his way down a very tricky track late at night. He rode the centerline all the way down but safely kept it in his lane to meet up with his father in the final. WJ won that one.

May 20, 1994, was a monumental day in the history of drag racing as Kurt Johnson recorded the first sub-7-second run in the history of Pro Stock. He earned the first Holley 6-second club trophy for his 6.988-second pass recorded at Englishtown. "I've always felt comfortable as a driver," said KJ. "I used to swim in high school, and it's a lot like that. You get in the pool, and you're all by yourself. You slam the doors on a race car, and it's just you."

On Sunday morning before Englishtown eliminations, KJ was awarded the $25,000 check for his record-breaking 6.988.

Just a handful of days later, the team arrived in Topeka, and KJ's confidence was high.

"I was like, alright, a good track, look out," he admitted.

There was an unexpected curveball, though, when the alcohol dragsters and Funny Cars ran ahead of Pro Stock and dispensed a magnitude of oil and caused multiple delays. The surface had been cleaned and scrubbed, but

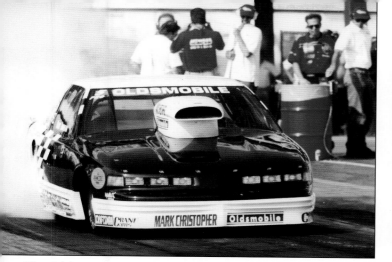

The Olds Cutlass driven by KJ in 1995 was a perfect 2 for 2 in final rounds. When asked if he agreed with his father that he possesses a natural mechanical aptitude, KJ said, "I can figure things out. I can fix stuff. It's more of a confidence builder than anything, knowing I can analyze an issue and find a solution for it." (Photo Courtesy Les Welch Family)

KJ gets a little camera time after securing the pole at Heartland Park. He was a two-time No. 1 qualifier in 1995 and scored the honor in both Sonoma and Topeka that season. (Photo Courtesy Les Welch Family)

Q&A with Arlene Johnson

Q: Did you always have a feeling Kurt would be involved in the race program?

A: I didn't imagine he would be this involved. We told him he could do what he wanted to do, and there were a couple of things he talked about doing after high school, but this is what he chose.

Q: When both Kurt and Warren were driving, were you ever worried about safety?

A: Oh, no. It's more dangerous to drive out on the street than it is out on the racetrack. You have all the safety equipment protecting you. I never worried about them.

Q: How did you decide which lane to stand in when they raced one another?

A: When Kurt started driving, I would video Warren's car because I felt he knew more about driving by the seat of your pants than Kurt. Warren was still the breadwinner.

Q: Were they competitive?

A: Oh yes, but it was never a problem. They ran the same equipment, everything was built here the same way, Kurt ran the dyno on all the engines. It was never a problem as far as any big disputes, but they didn't always agree on everything. If Warren said the sky was black, Kurt would say it was white.

Q: Are there any moments that stand out for you in which you were particularly proud of Kurt?

A: He won Seattle and then two more the first year he raced. He has 40 wins, which I think is pretty good. Had we been able to keep going, he would probably have more. He came close to winning the championship so

"Arlene was a big part of their racing operation," said NHRA's National Dragster Editor Phil Burgess, who covered WJ from the beginning. "If nothing else, she was always there to keep the boys straight. It was always cool to see this family doing everything on their own and taking it to the big boys."

many times, but it just didn't happen.

Q: How about with Warren, what moments stand out as ones that you're really proud of?

A: Probably winning his first championship, then of course winning Indy. Back when we won Indy the first few times, it was the race to win. Winning was always great, but winning Indy was it. There was nothing like it.

Les Lovett (left) with KJ. Lovett, a famed and beloved NHRA photographer, lost his life in 1996. He was responsible for many of the early images of KJ in the pages of National Dragster. (Photo Courtesy Auto Imagery)

it was not the same as it had been when they had arrived. KJ had been able to drive the centerline so well in Noble, though, that he had faith in his still-developing ability.

His previous command of a race car in suspect conditions did not translate to Topeka though. In his first tour down the drag strip at Heartland Park, KJ was riding the centerline again but this time, he lost control and wrecked.

"I was mad, and my pride was injured," he said. "But I just jumped back in the

The Professor's Way: Lesson 24

"I was the first Pro Stocker to run a two-car team when I had Scott Geoffrion driving for a while, and I saw the opportunity there," Warren Johnson said. "If you have two cars under your control, you have eight runs worth of data while everybody else only has four. Data acquisition back then was mostly by the seat of your pants. It was pretty crude. Having two cars gave us the opportunity to be more competitive on Sunday than the others."

KJ finished fourth in the NHRA Winston Pro Stock standings in 1996 just before his wife, Kathy, gave birth to their first child, Conner. The day after their son was born, GM Service Parts Operations announced a three-year extension of their sponsorship agreement. KJ's Pontiac Firebird wore sleek ACDelco Freedom Battery branding in the season of his first major sponsorship. That's John Pluchinco in the far lane. (Photo Courtesy Les Welch Family)

ESPN reporter Gary Gerould interviews KJ at the top end after the Las Vegas win in 2006. KJ finished No. 5 that season with three wins in a total of four final rounds. In addition to the Vegas victory, he also won Chicago and Memphis. (Photo Courtesy Auto Imagery)

Racing wasn't the only thing that marked the decade as a successful one. In 1996, it also included the birth of WJ's first grandchild, Conner, who is seen here with his dad KJ and WJ. Within the next few years, Kurt and wife, Kathy, welcomed daughter Erin and son Jarrett. Although none of KJ's three children opted to go the racing route, they each made memories at the racetrack while growing up. (Photo Courtesy Auto Imagery)

Scribner car I had crashed at Phoenix for Q2."

Harry Scribner's car had been repaired since the damaging Phoenix mishap, and he had brought it to Topeka to race. When KJ came to him in need, Scribner forfeited his seat to his friend who was chasing the points and making a grand showing in the Rookie of the Year contest.

The grateful Johnson team extracted the engine from their wrecked Pro Stocker and bolted it into Scribner's Olds Cutlass. KJ didn't miss a run that weekend until bowing out in the semifinals.

The highlight of the 1994 season for the Johnson family was, without a doubt, the 6.988-second pass that KJ made in Englishtown on May 20. It was the first sub-7-second pass in the history of the class, and the Dodge Boys had been breathing down their necks in the race to get there first. KJ didn't win a race or even reach a final round that season, but to blaze the trail into the 6s was a badge of honor he would wear for his entire career.

A short time after reaching the monumental milestone, though, KJ wrecked the record-setting car, and that was where Dad drew the line.

"I sent him to Bondurant [High Performance Driving School] to learn car control, and that made a driver out of him," said WJ. "We were running on iffy tracks, and Kurt saw me save a lot of runs that very few other people could have saved. He thought he'd know how to do it because he'd seen it so much, but I had the advantage of learning how to race on ice and snow. The school turned him right around. To this day, he is still one of the best drivers out there."

KJ's 1997 ride was the red, white, and blue ACDelco Pontiac Firebird. He won Brainerd, Indy, and the NHRA Finals that season and finished No. 3 in the Pro Stock points. "One thing instilled in the beginning, when Kurt first started driving, was that if you make mistakes, it's probably because you were excited," said WJ. "It wasn't a problem because he's basically unflappable." (Photo Courtesy Evan J. Smith)

A Quick Study

Kurt has been known to confess that the 1993 season seemed almost easy, despite a handful of jarring experiences. He stepped into a program that was already equipped with a significant performance advantage over

At St. Louis in 1999, KJ was the Pro Stock No. 1 qualifier. It was one of four starts for KJ from the top spot that year in a season in which his father would be crowned the world champ. The younger Johnson won three times in five final rounds that year to finish No. 3 in the Pro Stock points. (Photo Courtesy Auto Imagery)

KJ is in the driver's seat of his ACDelco-branded Chevrolet in 2005. He qualified for every race he attempted from his debut in 1993 on through the first three years of full-time racing. (Photo Courtesy Auto Imagery)

KJ and Greg Anderson (left) remained friends despite Anderson's departure to start his own team. Here they are at the top end at the 2005 fall race in Las Vegas after KJ defeated his friendly rival in the final round. When Anderson came to WJ and told him that he was thinking about making the move to drive a car of his own, WJ recalled, "Well, I thought it was fine. He stayed another year after that, probably because looking at the financial end of it, he realized he would be without a paycheck so he better figure out how to structure that. The reality of no paycheck was probably pretty daunting. But I didn't have any problems when he left. He was doing his thing, and I was doing mine. If he learned enough here to be successful, then my part of the equation was complete." (Photo Courtesy Auto Imagery)

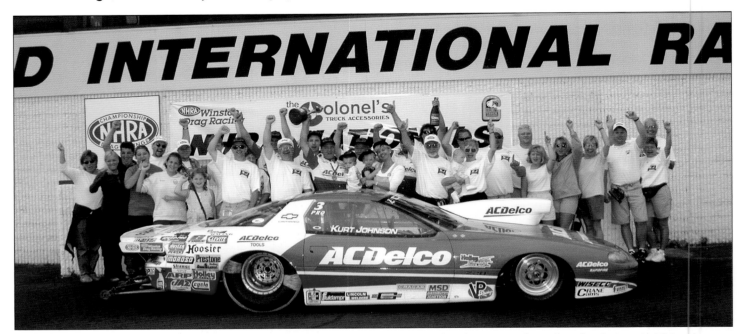

There were four wins for KJ at Brainerd International Raceway, his family's home track, in five final rounds. This photo was taken in the Brainerd winner's circle in 2000, the year KJ beat Jeg Coughlin Jr. in the final round. KJ and Jeg raced each another eight times for the trophy, and Kurt held a 7-1 advantage at last count. (Photo Courtesy Auto Imagery)

most of the teams, and the horsepower continued to develop and grow. All of the pieces were in place. There was still plenty to study, but KJ was ready to learn.

Every season seemed to produce its share of rewards for the amiable racer who balanced a laid-back vibe with an obviously inherited, admirable work ethic. Three wins in his rookie season, the 6.988 record pass in his second year, and then at least one win for 14 consecutive seasons (from 1995 until 2008) continued to fuel his motivation.

In 1996, KJ gained sponsorship from ACDelco, and he retained its support for the majority of his Pro Stock driving career. His father piloted the Pontiac brand after the Olds program went away, and KJ

Kurt and wife Kathy in 1992. They both hail from Minnesota and built a life and family together in Georgia, where they continue to reside. At the time, KJ was crew chief for the Team II car with Don Beverley at the wheel. "The more you get into it, the more you want to do it," said KJ, of being a crew chief. "You kind of grow on your own. It just keeps getting bigger and bigger and better and better."

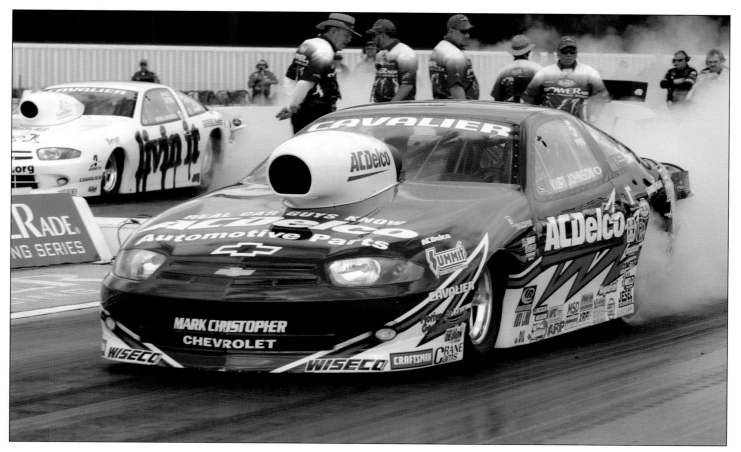

The ACDelco Chevrolet Cobalt as piloted by KJ in 2005 at the season-opening NHRA Winternationals. KJ clocked low ET and top speed of the meet with his 6.692-second pass paired with a 206.35-mph speed. (Photo Courtesy Auto Imagery)

WJ and KJ are on the starting line with Matt Hartford, who was using their horsepower in his Pro Stock car. Hartford didn't win a round the season before, but with the Johnson family's engine and expertise, he was able to reach the semifinals by Sonoma in 2016. (Photo Courtesy Auto Imagery)

WJ teaches his grandkids Conner and Erin the racing ropes in 2001.

wheeled Chevrolet vehicles to dole out a wicked double dose of Warren Johnson power on behalf of General Motors.

From 1995 until 2008, KJ brought home 36 of his 40 overall wins, most impressively raking in 6 trophies in 6 final rounds in 2000. He won the prestigious U.S. Nationals twice (1996 and 1997), and the Pro Stock all-star bonus race four times. In all, he was the No. 1 qualifier at 29 events and reset 5 national records.

At the time of print, he was No. 2 on the list of drivers who had recorded the most wins without a world championship. He came awfully close, though, on four occasions. In each, he finished second in the Pro Stock standings—once to his father.

KJ said that like his father, he would be game to drive a Pro Stock car again one day, but only if they had sufficient funding to be competitive. (Note: Larry Morgan once said that if he won the lottery, he would personally fund the father-son Johnson revival tour.) If KJ does not return, his last win will have been at Minnesota's Brainerd International Raceway in 2008. It was a fitting location to call it a career for the Minnesota-born driver who developed a taste for drag racing in his own backyard.

These days, KJ is content to work alongside WJ at the shop, and he spends as much time as he can with his wife, Kathy, and their grown children Conner, Erin, and Jarrett.

KJ, shown here in 2006, was the NHRA's Rookie of the Year in 1993. His two most productive seasons were 2000, when he claimed six wins in six final rounds with four No. 1–qualifier awards, and 2003, when his elimination-round win-loss record was 49-18 with four wins in 10 finals. (Photo Courtesy Auto Imagery)

KJ's Biggest Rivals	
Opponent	Final-Round Record
Greg Anderson	3-14
Warren Johnson	2-11
Justin Humphreys	0-1
Jim Yates	4-4
Mike Edwards	3-3
Ron Krisher	1-0
Scott Geoffrion	1-0
Gene Wilson	1-0
Allen Johnson	1-0
Troy Coughlin Sr.	1-0
Tom Martino	1-0
V. Gaines	1-0
Rickie Smith	1-0
Robert Patrick	1-0
Mark Pawuk	1-0
Greg Stanfield	2-1
Darrell Alderman	2-0
Jason Line	3-2
Dave Connolly	4-2
Jeg Coughlin Jr.	7-1

CHAPTER 10

RESEARCH AND DEVELOPMENT

Warren Johnson was, and still is, very much a trailblazer. His development of the DRCE, as discussed in depth in chapter 5, brought Pro Stock to a new level of competition, and the reliable, efficient engine is still in use decades later.

The DRCE was most assuredly one of Johnson's greatest and most well-known accomplishments, but his research and development wasn't limited to engine blocks and cylinder heads.

Fuel Injection

WJ was a very early proponent of fuel injection for Pro Stock, and he firmly believed it was a necessary step to advance the class. When conversation arose pertaining to future performance barriers, WJ was keen to suggest that implementing electronic fuel injection (EFI) would be a logical progression. He argued that it would increase the life expectancy of the engine immensely (by

While WJ was adept at managing a carbureted fuel system, he was a big proponent of electronic fuel injection (EFI) and diligently spoke of the benefits long before it was mandated for Pro Stock in 2016.

approximately 35 to 40 percent) and that it would eliminate trace detonation. His assertions began many years before the NHRA technical department made the change to EFI for Pro Stock in 2016.

Shifting Gears

"My favorite WJ quote was him saying that the reason the NHRA rule book was double-spaced was so that he could write between the lines," said *National Dragster* Editor Phil Burgess. "There had to be a pioneer who was willing to get the arrows in the ass, and he was the perfect guy for it."

Though it was initially put to use in an admittedly clandestine manner in a very public setting, the Professor is noted for leading the way in the evolution of the Pro Stock transmission from a traditional 4-speed to a further-reaching, more capable 5-speed.

"I just wanted the extra gear ratio," he said. "The rule book didn't say it had to be a 4-speed transmission, just that it had to have three gear cases—three gear reduction plus a direct. I didn't take that to mean you couldn't split the gear ratios and actually shift a gear twice."

WJ is most comfortable with his mind and hands working with an engine, whether it's in the development and preparation process or in the engine compartment of his race car. His work with the DRCE was revolutionary and changed the heartbeat of Pro Stock. "If you can find 5 hp or a matter of 15 hp by the end of the year, you've made sizable gains, but those gains are hard to come by," said the Professor. "It costs a lot of money to find 5 hp."

On Sharing Information

Pro Stock is well known as the category with the most closely guarded proprietary secrets. Warren Johnson is more of a listener than a talker, so the chances of any information pertaining to a performance advantage ever slipping out were slim to none. However, he had something aside from a performance advantage that others wanted: knowledge.

"I would never go to my competitors with a question," said WJ. "You know flat-out they're going to lie or they don't know. Knowing that, I'd have to be awful stupid to ask any questions.

"When they came to me, if I felt it was a sensitive area or that we had proprietary information, I would just say that I didn't want to talk about it. But if I had common knowledge and they needed a little insight, I'd never lie to them. Just like I never cheated racing, I would help anybody out there who had a legitimate question. If they asked me something they should know, though, that would really irritate me. I'd just tell them, 'You obviously should know the answer, so why ask me?'

"I did get a lot of questions that made me a little concerned about their mental stability. Depending on the way a question was asked, it could make me think in a different light. I'd listen to anybody who had a concern about this or that, and there were a lot of cases where I'd stand back and say, 'You know, I didn't really think about it that way.'"

WJ leaned into research and development as he raced toward six championships. He wore the No. 2 on the window in eight seasons of NHRA Pro Stock competition (1976, 1984–1986, 1988, 1991, 1996, and 1997). (Photo Courtesy Evan J. Smith)

WJ's well-prepared Pontiac Grand Am in 2005 claimed three wins in five final rounds for a No. 4 finish in the Pro Stock points. (Photo Courtesy Auto Imagery)

At the time, there wasn't a sprag available that was robust enough to be upshifted, so WJ enlisted the help of people he knew in the industry who had a government contract to produce helicopter sprags. Their one-way mechanical clutches used a method of preventing the pinion from rotating backward while allowing the transmission to smoothly change gears under load.

WJ's theory was finding legs as he raced with his newly enhanced transmission at several events. In Seattle, an alarm was sounded for anyone paying attention. WJ didn't realize that the driver in the other lane was broke, and he took off down the quarter mile on an unexpected single.

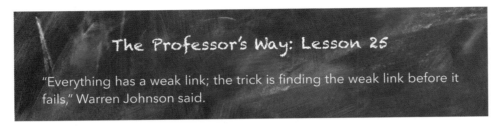

The 1985 Oldsmobile Calais that WJ had fabricator Willie Rells equip with a Funny Car–style steel roll cage is shown. WJ's impact in the safety of NHRA drag racing reached across many classes, and he was the first to attempt and implement a variety of safety measures that the NHRA would adopt. (Photo Courtesy Steve Reyes)

"They heard four gear changes instead of three, so NHRA came over to take a look at it," WJ said. "If you play dumb, you can get by with a lot of stuff. But it wasn't illegal, and I'm sure other people had thought of it, they just didn't understand how to do it."

The tech department didn't think it was dumb at all, and the 5-gear transmission was made legal soon after. WJ still held an advantage, though, because his style of 5-speed was a four-case version and weighed approximately 110 pounds. His competitors went the route of bolting on an additional case, which made the transmission 40 pounds heavier.

"That's just too big of an alligator to be wrestling inside the car," said the ever-efficient WJ.

Safety Measures

WJ has been quite vocal in terms of his insistence upon safety in Pro Stock and drag racing in general. He has never hesitated to voice his opinion on the safety of a racetrack, no matter the circumstances, and his efforts to make drag racing as safe as possible extended beyond concern over the racing surface.

At the Cajun Nationals in Baton Rouge in 1985, WJ witnessed the fatal crash of Pro Stock driver Mickey Tadlock. There were no mandates for roll cages or shoulder harnesses at that time, and WJ was deeply impacted by what he saw. Without hesitation, he booked a flight to San Diego to meet with Willie Rells, the fabricator who was just beginning to build his new Calais for competition.

Roll Cage

WJ showed Rells precisely how he wanted him to incorporate a Funny Car–style high-strength steel roll cage into the Calais for stability, including dual-mount shoulder harnesses. This equipment could have potentially saved Tadlock's life.

Every one of WJ's Pro Stockers from then on incorporated every possible safety measure. His vision and strides in the area of safety have had a positive impact on the lives of thousands of drivers across the sport.

Jerry Haas and Don Ness were among the first car builders to join WJ in adopting the use of the upgraded safety features. The NHRA's technical department was receptive, spelling out the new safety features in the rule book and making the roll cage and, eventually, dual-mount shoulder harnesses standard equipment for a Pro Stock chassis.

Beadlock Wheel

After a series of wrecks by his competitors prior to the 2004 season, WJ was part of a series of tire tests. He worked with the manufacturer to come up with a beadlock rear wheel design to replace what was, in essence, a handful of sheet-metal screws attaching the tire to the wheel. The rigid assembly of the beadlock wheel provided lateral stability to reduce tire shake. With the new design for the rear tires, the power was more safely transferred to the ground and performance was increased.

Dual Parachutes and Seat Designs

WJ was also instrumental in the incorporation of dual parachutes.

"That was something we worked on with Stroud Safety because I saw so many failed deployments of parachutes," he said. "By adding a second parachute, you double your

The Professor's Way: Lesson 26

"I have a preconceived idea of what I'm trying to accomplish, but because I think outside the box so much, that can change when a different material comes along," Warren Johnson said. "For example, we might change a casting so that I can do something else with cylinder head design. It's a constant moving target. You're looking at it and working on it until you find something one day."

chances of getting safely stopped. We also revised the seat design after Brandon Bernstein's [Top Fuel] accident. You need performance, but at the same time, you need an equal helping of safety. These cars just go too quick and too fast to not take safety into consideration."

GM's Secret Weapon

When the original agreement with Oldsmobile came about and WJ took over on the DRCE project, it opened up access to what he was really interested in: research and development. WJ considered that his real forte.

He was less concerned with the bodystyle they requested he run because he surmised that as long as he put enough power underneath the hood, he could make any car competitive. His theory was proven repeatedly as he set speed records with even the least aerodynamic of vehicles, including the Hurst/Olds, which he endearingly referred to as the "flying boxcar."

His partnership with General Motors was a win-win from the start. As much as he represented the brand on an exceptional level in terms of high performance, he was able to grow his operation and expand his education by leaps and bounds.

"The sponsor money from GM was enough that I could invest in my operation," explained WJ. "The multiyear contracts allowed me to forecast what I would be able to do based on the amount of money I was going to receive, and if I was successful at winning races, then I could augment that income. Part of my agreement with them was that I had to supply so many engineering hours, and that allowed me to intermingle with GM engineers and work on projects that really interested me both in and outside of drag racing."

Throughout the 1990s, a decade of true dominance, WJ noted that there weren't any large advancements that impacted their performance. It was just a matter of chipping away at small things, and it was an endless task.

The concepts were still the same, he was just able to zero in on different areas of potential improvement in terms of materials and design. It was an evolution that required an open mind all the time. A performance increase could come from something as miniscule as a

titanium valve keeper; while everyone else was using steel, WJ had already been using titanium for nearly 10 years.

WJ believes that he gained the most success by keeping his finger on the pulse of not only new technology but also materials. As a lifelong student of engineering, he was obsessed with the new materials that were becoming increasingly available.

"Only two things can contribute to performance increase in any category: how much you think about performance and how much you think about and invest in new materials," WJ said. "Valve springs, camshafts,

Engine work wasn't only performed at the race shop. WJ would address whatever needed to be attended to on the road. Here he is, elbow deep in the engine, at a national event.

Fueled for Development

Steve Burns founded VP Racing Fuels in 1975 and sought the best minds in the racing industry to help him with testing and development. A racer himself, Burns turned to Pro Stock engine builders and racers, including Reher-Morrison, Bob Glidden, and Warren Johnson.

WJ was actually his first official paying customer and became instrumental in advancements for the company. Their initial connection came when WJ called Burns after seeing an ad in *National Dragster*. Burns recalled that WJ drilled him with questions.

"He asked more questions than anyone, ever, over the span of about 30 years," marveled Burns, who immediately recognized that there was potential for an effective collaboration.

Burns traveled to WJ's shop, towing a horse trailer loaded with fuel components that he wished to test for effectiveness. WJ allowed him to bring his "mobile lab" and use the dyno, and KJ assisted their guest scientist.

"I remember one night it was Kurt and myself, and we started playing with fuels and making dyno runs," recalled Burns. "We would establish a baseline and then make significant changes. We were running this thing into the ground—we were basically kids who didn't want to stop.

"Kurt and I worked all night long, and Warren came in the next morning and we handed him the dyno reports. He looked at it, and we didn't have the 10 or 15 horsepower that he'd said would be good, we had 15 or 20 horsepower and better torque. He just looked at it and said, 'Yeah, okay,' and handed it back. So, I said, 'Okay? This is just okay?' And he said, 'Well, that's what you came

Take a secret look at the workspace within the race trailer. Many hours were logged by WJ and his crew in this space as they whittled away at their program, making changes both large and small between qualifying rounds and then hustling to complete necessary maintenance between elimination rounds. "Clutch is really a key element in these cars," said WJ. "It's a high-service item that has got be serviced every round. As the cars become more and more technical, it became a lot harder to maintain between rounds in that small time frame. We used every minute available between rounds."

here to do, isn't it?' Then he turned around and walked off.

"But that's just how he was. Warren was really factual, and he always made me think. I would say that he helped form me into who I am today."

anywhere you can improve the performance with better materials, that's what we did. It wasn't restricted to engines; now it was shock absorbers and Goodyear continually working on R&D to produce better tires. Every-

thing on the car should be there helping it to win, not holding it back."

WJ formed acquaintanceships with a variety of individuals over the years, not just in racing but in many walks of life where engineers reside. A partnership with a manufacturer of one piece might have led to any

The 190-mph target was on the mind of everyone in the class, but WJ got there first in his Oldsmobile Firenza at the 1986 U.S. Nationals in Indianapolis. He clocked a brisk 190.07 that held the record for speed for a full year. "It was a typical Indy, hot and humid, and I honestly didn't expect to run 190 there," said WJ. "But we had changed so many parts in that Firenza engine-wise, and it seemed to be getting better. It kind of surprised us though. Back then, I didn't even have a dyno." (Photo Courtesy Steve Reyes)

number of individuals becoming available to bounce ideas off of or learn from. Ever the student himself, WJ gobbled up information about new, stronger, and lighter materials that could benefit his program.

"It was a constant program of trying to source better materials," he said. "I didn't limit it to this country either. I would search overseas if I had to. It was always, 'How can I get this, or can I substitute something else for it?'"

Thinking outside the box was WJ's forte, and it served him well. He was fixated on machining and answering even the smallest of queries, such as which bearings were best for spindles, because he also wanted to know how that application might apply to another area, so he would expand his system of testing in that direction.

WJ tested rolling resistance in a car and worked to find the answer when it was too high. He particularly thrived on examining and improving aerodynamics. While his competitors were struggling with GM's J-Body, WJ dug deep with his own (the Goodwrench Performance Parts Olds Firenza) and pushed it to be the first Pro Stocker to eclipse 190 mph.

"It was all built within the NHRA rules, plus or minus an inch, of course," he laughed.

Car Talk

WJ stated many times that he wasn't particularly fond of any of the race cars that he piloted. It wasn't that he didn't like them, he just had no interest in aesthetics. He enjoyed the challenge of making any car go fast. To him, a car was just a tool and nothing to get sentimental over. If something about the car didn't jive with WJ's thought process, he'd grab a torch and a hammer.

The question of favorites has been a common question for the Professor, and his standard reply is generally a variation of, "I'd race a John Deere tractor if it could win Pro Stock. It doesn't make a difference to me what kind of car it is; the engine can't read the name on the hood anyway."

WJ believes that the only real reason to hold on to a car is for what it holds in historical value. The Firebird

The Professor's Way: Lesson 27

"On an ideal race car, you aren't hauling anything along that you don't need," Warren Johnson said. "Everything has a function. Everything. If it doesn't add to the performance of the vehicle, it's not required. Remember, it's a drag race, not a car show. Don't spend an excessive amount of time waxing and polishing."

WJ knew what he wanted to achieve with the Vega build, but he simply didn't have time to bring his vision to life between the demands of going to school and working full time. He was quite impressed with George Wepplo's implementation of his ideas and his masterful construction. "The Vega was actually a pretty stable car," said WJ. "It was extremely lightweight–probably one of the lightest ever built with a big-block and manual 4-speed in it." (Photo Courtesy Ray-Mar/Randy Henning)

that made the first 200-mph Pro Stock pass is on loan to the Motorsports Hall of Fame of America in Daytona.

Early on, WJ determined that he didn't have time to build his own cars, although he had the desire and will. Toward the beginning of his career, he enlisted the assistance of fabricator George Wepplo to build the wily Vega, and the car was masterfully stitched together from the ground up with just body panels and tubing.

Many of WJ's cars in the early years were built by Don Ness. Minnesota chassis builder Ness set the bar on quality and design in Pro Stock, according to WJ. In 1971, WJ fielded a Camaro that was one of the first Ness Pro Stockers to be incorporated with torsion bars in the rear suspension.

Veteran builder Willie Rells produced one of WJ's early Oldsmobiles, and Rick Jones built a few for WJ here and there. It was primarily esteemed builder Jerry Haas who fabricated the bulk of the Warren Johnson Enterprises entries in the last decade and a half of its racing endeavors.

More than a chassis builder, Haas has also been a Pro Stock racer himself, so he understands the car on a very intimate level. He was a three-time finalist in the now-defunct Pro Stock Truck category and built and raced Pro Stock cars from 1973 to 1995.

WJ commissioned George Wepplo to build the Chevrolet Vega from the ground up. (Photo Courtesy Ray-Mar/Randy Henning)

"When we got the chance to work with WJ, we were very grateful," said Haas from his Jerry Haas Race Cars shop in Fenton, Missouri. "Back in the 1980s and early 1990s, he was just light-years ahead of everybody else in technology."

WJ corralled his car builders into acting as another branch of research and development. He would come to them with ideas of design, and the chassis builder would implement them. If the idea produced results, WJ requested a one-year moratorium on the builder's use of the idea for other customers. After that, it was game on.

"It was kind of like lawyer/client privilege or doctor/patient confidentiality," explained Haas. "It was really awesome working with Warren because our company learned a lot from it. I think he learned from us too. It was a win-win situation for both of us."

Pro Stock 30-Year Evolution										
Year Specifications	Make	Performance	Engine	Horsepower	Torque	Vehicle Weight	Chassis	Body	Wheelbase	Cost
1975	Chevrolet Camaro	8.79 seconds/ 155 mph	393-ci Chevrolet big-block V-8	800	650 ft-lbs	2,830 pounds	Chrome moly steel tubing	Factory steel with fiberglass hood and fenders	108 inches	$70,000
2005	Pontiac Grand Am	6.715 seconds/ 205.69 mph	500-ci GM DRCE-3	1,360 (at 9,400 rpm)	830 ft-lbs (at 8,000 rpm)	2,350 pounds (with driver)	Chrome moly steel tubing	Carbon fiber/Kevlar composite	105 inches	$350,000

This data is shown as it was printed in the GM Performance Parts Warren Johnson 2005 Media Guide.

The relationship that WJ fostered with General Motors provided the engineer both financial stability and a viable reason to cater to his desire to dig deep into all aspects of the race car from engine blocks to chassis design. The win-win partnership netted well over 100 wins when KJ's victories for the team are factored in. (Photo Courtesy Auto Imagery)

Because of WJ's partnership with General Motors and his extensive delve into aerodynamics and horsepower, quite a few race cars have wandered through his garage. Turning back the clock to the beginning of his appreciation for power and speed, however, reveals that he'd never settled on one car for too long. He had 1940, 1948, and 1949 Chevys, a couple of Tri-Five Chevrolets (including the '57 in which he won his first bracket race), and a 1966 Chevelle in the earliest days. Those classic Bowtie hot rods were followed by a series of increasingly powerful Camaros.

WJ had his squirrely little Vega that did double-duty in AHRA Pro Stock and NHRA B/A, and then came Jerome Bradford's Monte Carlo, the Starfire in which he claimed his first NHRA win, the Firenza that broke 190 mph, and of course the classic black and silver Hurst/Olds that forever cemented WJ's name and likeness in the Oldsmobile Drag Racing program.

The Calais years followed, and then the Cutlass and Cutlass Supreme entries came on the scene. GM Performance Pontiacs were the order of the latter days of WJ's career and included the Firebird, Grand Am, GTO, and GXP models. WJ's final Pro Stocker was a Jerry Haas–built Pontiac GXP that he was still utilizing for research and development at his shop in 2020.

The Competition Engine Service Inc. Chevy Camaro, shown here in 1971 at Minnesota Dragways, was really a vehicle that allowed WJ to bring his ever-sharpening engineering skills into the Pro Stock forum. "The way I look at a race car, everything has to contribute to the performance of that vehicle. My focus was on every detail that related to how we could make the car more efficient. My race cars would never win a car show, but we weren't at a car show, we were at a race." (Photo Courtesy John Foster Jr.)

CHAPTER 11

COMFORTABLE WITH CONTROVERSY

For those who have followed Pro Stock, a mention of Warren Johnson perhaps does not evoke a warm, fuzzy feeling, unless prolific accomplishments make your heart flutter. He is a brilliant engineer and an absolute visionary, an inarguably legendary engine builder, and one of the most deservedly decorated drivers of all time—and not just in Pro Stock, in any category.

WJ was a controversial character throughout his career, though, because he says what he thinks and is completely unafraid of who will hear it.

"He was right 99 percent of the time, and there was never anything that he complained about that didn't need to be complained about," said drag racing veteran Larry Morgan, who joined the Pro Stock contingent in 1987. "Warren wasn't afraid or intimidated to say what he thought, and most of the time he said what he did because he wanted to make sure that the racing was safe. There were times when the track wasn't good, and we would make the run but know that there were guys behind us who weren't as experienced and could be in trouble. That's the kind of stuff he would talk about, and he was right to do it."

In 2009, WJ and Morgan raced one another in the first round of eliminations at the 25th annual Toyo Tires NHRA Nationals at Maple Grove Raceway in Reading, Pennsylvania. It was the 56th time the two had lined up next to one another on race day in NHRA competition, and it came after a wicked bout of rain had plagued the area and wreaked havoc with the racing surface. Unfortunately, moisture had built up beneath the racing surface and began seeping out just as the Pro Stock cars (with very little downforce) were called forth.

One of the cars in the pair before WJ and Morgan got quite loose at the top end, and safety officials worked to rectify the situation for about 30 minutes. Once given the go-ahead, the seasoned veterans did their burnouts and staged. WJ left first by a smidge and kept the advantage, but as he got down track and moved through fourth and fifth gears, his Pontiac GXP encountered a series of puddles and began to skate erratically. WJ drove it like a pro and got it safely stopped, but he was livid at the top end.

"This has been a longtime problem," WJ told ESPN's Gary Gerould. "It's probably manifested itself worse in the last few years, simply from the fact the NHRA as a sanctioning body hasn't been paying due diligence to what they should be doing instead of just scalping the spectators. What's happened is the fact they didn't slow those Fuel cars down 5 or 10 years ago as they should have

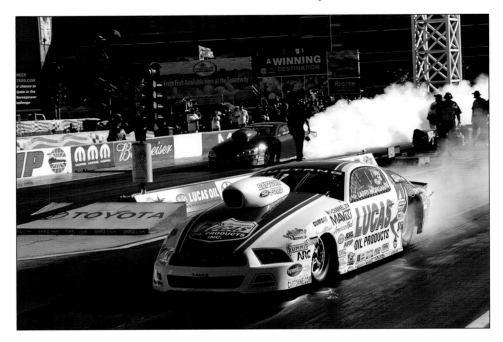

In Las Vegas in 2013, WJ was with Larry Morgan (near lane), who joined the Pro Stock fraternity in 1987. The two became good friends over the years and remained friends long after both had vacated the driver's seat. WJ and Morgan raced one another in the final round eight times with WJ winning five of their money-round matches. Both were vocal when they observed injustice. Morgan was credited with using the phrase "You can't fix stupid" to describe the sanctioning body's management of Pro Stock, and fans loved it, showing up to the next event wearing T-shirts with the quote. (Photo Courtesy Auto Imagery)

by having a tech committee that was cognizant of what was going on.

"If they would have slowed them down, the tracks wouldn't have to be spending four or five hundred thousand dollars just for shut-off areas for only 32 cars in the whole country. Less than 1/10 of 1 percent of all the drag racing cars in this country are going to ruin this sport. I'm sure after this telecast there's going to be some dialog between all of the competitors—with the exception of Fuel cars—with the NHRA because it's something that needs to be addressed before somebody gets killed out there."

There were times when safety wasn't a factor in WJ's vocalizations, however. He simply understood an aspect of the sport that is often overlooked by drivers who are narrowly focused.

"Once I started racing full time, it didn't take me two or three years to figure out that this is nothing but entertainment," said WJ. "If you can introduce some enter-

The Professor's Way: Lesson 29

"I never felt like I had to prove anything to anybody," Warren Johnson said. "There was nothing to prove. I was just trying to make a living."

tainment that people aren't expecting, that's just a plus for the spectators. So, that's what I did."

WJ participated in some spectacularly well-known burndowns at the starting line (more on this in chapter 8) and sometimes had some pretty choice words for competitors at the top end, but it was all part of the program.

That didn't make it any easier, though, for the individuals harnessed with handling his public relations over the years.

Proper Representation

Rick Voegelin, an award-winning author and widely respected writer and publicist in the automotive and high-performance world, knew of WJ well before they crossed paths.

"I was very aware of him, of course, while I was working at Petersen Publishing," said Voegelin, who was the editor of *Car Craft* magazine at the time. "The staff there was made up of really hardcore racer types and drag racing enthusiasts. I was part of the hardcore doorslammer set."

Voegelin left the magazine at the end of 1979 and launched a business of his own in freelance writing, which eventually morphed into advertising and public relations. Oldsmobile was one of the clients that he acquired, and that was when his working relationship with WJ took place. WJ was the face of the brand's drag racing program in the late 1980s and 1990s, and as the manager of Oldsmobile Motorsports drag racing public relations branch, Voegelin spent a lot of time speaking with and gathering information about WJ.

He put together press kits, releases, pit notes, and any marketing material that he was called upon to produce. The two related on a technical level and, according to Voegelin, "spoke the same language." Even so, there was always a certain level of challenge when it came to representing the Professor.

But there were times when WJ's expressive opinion outside of the mechanics of race cars created situations that were tough to smooth over in terms of public relations. Once, WJ said to a television reporter that then-NHRA President Dallas Gardner only hired people dumber than he was. At the next race, a group showed

WJ on Being Controversial

"I was just trying to advance the sport, which would help both competitors and the NHRA. Whether it fell on deaf ears, I can't control. But I look at the big picture. We have entertainment here, we have spectators there, we better make this thing work. With the egos of the management and their silk suits, I think a lot of times they didn't accept that."

Johnson in 2011. (Photo Courtesy Auto Imagery)

Fan Interaction

At the end of each day of racing, WJ set aside time to spend with the fans. While some drivers pepper their day with time at the ropes mingling with spectators, WJ was the central figure in making sure that his race program and all of its elements were operating at 100 percent. He had to remain focused to continue to run his business, the business of drag racing for a living. Fans were always welcome to stand at the ropes and observe the operation at any time, but WJ let them know, by way of a sign on the back of the trailer, that he would be available to them once the activities of the day had concluded. This wasn't always well-received or understood, but WJ felt that he had found a way to balance the important aspects of his job.

"Fans were always important to me," said WJ. "I would spend time with them at the end of the day, sign autographs, talk to them, every day. That never changed from when I first started racing until the last day I raced. I knew that if the fans weren't there, the sponsors weren't there. If the sponsors weren't there, then the racers aren't going to be there either. You have to realize that if the fans aren't entertained, they might go bowling."

WJ at the ropes with fans after qualifying. (Photo Courtesy Les Welch Family)

A young fan gets an autograph from the Professor after qualifying had concluded. WJ carefully divided his time, giving his full attention to his race car during the day and enjoying time with the fans once the workday was through.

WJ spends time with a group of fans after qualifying. It was a good evening, as he was No. 1 qualifier there in Memphis in 1998 with a 6.881-second ET that allowed him to capture the 100th No. 1-qualifying position of his career. The following day, WJ went on to defeat KJ in the final round and claim his 72nd national event win trophy.

WJ versus Rickie Smith at the Pomona NHRA Winternationals in 1985. Smith, who also raced in the IHRA and was one of WJ's formidable competitors, was just as outspoken as the Professor, if not more. "One of the things that I recognized early on was that we're here for the entertainment of the fans," said WJ. "It was always more than just racing." (Photo Courtesy Steve Reyes)

Fans held a banner up for WJ in protest of the switch to Pontiac. He won the 1992, 1993, and 1995 championships in an Oldsmobile—the brand he had been affiliated with since he built the Starfire for the 1982 season. Ultimately, the brand shift came when Oldsmobile's drag racing program no longer suited the group's marketing vision, and GM opted to put its winning driver in a Pontiac.

"I admire Warren," said Steve Burns, founder of VP Racing Fuel. "Only a select few have been able to beat their way to the top of professional racing by just hard work and the support of their family. He did it without big money." (Photo Courtesy Auto Imagery)

up wearing T-shirts that proclaimed they were "Dumber than Dallas."

He frequently referred to the nitro Top Fuel dragsters as "horizontal oil derricks" and claimed that "even Ray Charles could drive a Fuel car." WJ was often at odds with the rule makers as he worked to find the next level of power within the confines of the rule book, and he also wasn't shy about stating his opinion on the condition of any given racetrack.

"He was very opinionated and spoke his mind, but Warren is extremely intelligent," said Voegelin. "He wasn't always great when it came to dealing with people, but he has a brilliant mind. I always believed that the moniker 'the Professor' really fit Warren. It wasn't just a marketing thing; he really was the Professor of Pro Stock. It said a lot about how he lived his life."

Little Sister

The husband-and-wife publicist team of Jon and Joanne Knapp were part of a firm in the 1990s that worked with Pro Stock driver Tom Martino. Martino and his then-wife, Robin, were good friends with KJ and his wife, Kathy. Through the Martino family, the Knapps met the Johnsons. Years later, the Knapps would become the lead publicists on the GM account, then held by TMG Sports Marketing, which would afford them an extended opportunity to represent both KJ and WJ and get to know them on a personal level.

"I remember when Tommy [Martino] won Brainerd, we went out to celebrate, and Warren and Arlene were there," recalled Joanne. "They were all telling stories, and one was about Warren doing a hayride in Houston for Halloween. I thought, 'Well, maybe he does have a normal side to him.' To us, he had always been 'the Professor,' but that was the first time I saw a different side to him. He is an absolute panic; so funny. Deep down inside, he's just a normal person. He can get grouchy, but so can anyone."

Working with WJ was a rich experience, and the Knapps were never left unentertained, although sometimes even the entertainment was a bit challenging.

"He was really easy to get a quote from," said Joanne. "But I'll never forget the first time I said, 'Warren, can I borrow you for a minute?' and he started counting down, '59, 58, 57, 56 . . .' Usually when I would walk in, he would look at me like, 'Smiley, what do you want?' He had numerous nicknames for me; one was *Munchkin*, and I don't have a clue how he gave me that."

In a sense, WJ's relationship with Joanne was almost sibling-like. He was like a big brother teasing his little sister at every available opportunity.

"One year, we were with them in the Zoo," recalled Joanne, referring to the rambunctious campground at Brainerd International Raceway that comes alive each

Jon and Joanne Knapp, in the winner's circle with WJ in Houston in 2005, represented both WJ and KJ, pitching them to media and coordinating interviews as well as writing press releases and managing additional marketing efforts on behalf of GM Performance. They had plenty to write about after the Houston event, where the Professor added an unusual distinction to his lengthy resume by qualifying in the No. 1 position and recording the 93rd win of his NHRA Pro Stock career, thus becoming the oldest professional winner in NHRA history. (Photo Courtesy Auto Imagery)

One of the most controversial "hot spots" on the NHRA tour was the Brainerd Zoo—the campground at Brainerd International Raceway where loads of fans carry on a four-day-long party complete with free-flowing booze, bonfires, fireworks, and layers of scandal that only sometimes are spoken of the next day. Some may be surprised to learn that Warren and Arlene never missed a trip to the Zoo.

A look at the staging lanes from above at Brainerd International Raceway in 1992. WJ got his start racing at various facilities in and around his home state of Minnesota, and by 1992 he was already standing out as a very distinct character in the sport.

evening after the racing events have concluded. "It started raining, so I put up the umbrella, and he told me to hold it higher and maybe lightning would strike. He was always giving me a hard time like that."

Joanne and Jon both enjoyed the banter and often dealt it right back. Once when WJ's luggage was left behind, the Knapps prepared a makeshift overnight bag to get him through until his things arrived the next day. They picked up a child's decorative hairbrush and toothbrush, security blanket, and Valentine's Day–themed boxers and socks adorned with hearts and kiss marks. When they brought it to WJ's hotel room, he rolled his eyes and accused them of having too much time on their hands.

"It's funny. I realize what he's accomplished, what he's done for drag racing and GM, his knowledge of an engine, and the DRCE-1, -2, -3," said Joanne. "It's amazing what he knows and what he's done. But Warren and Arlene became our friends. Even when we weren't contracted to work with them anymore, we would still talk to them, and we would still go out and do things together."

Their continued friendship is of particular interest because the next account that they acquired was with Greg Anderson, Johnson's protégé turned rival competitor. Many in the community assumed the new assignment would create bad blood, but it really never did.

"When the contract for Warren and Kurt went [unexpectedly to another firm] in 2009, it was like, 'What do we do now?'" said Joanne. "It was a week and a half before the first race of the year, we already had tickets to get there and a hotel room. So, we went anyway, and Warren and Arlene knew we were looking for a job. They understood.

"The first time I went over there [to the Johnsons' pit area after being contracted to work with Anderson and his Summit Racing teammate, Jason Line], I covered up the logo on my shirt and asked if they were still going

WJ and fellow Pro Stock racer and engine builder Tom Martino in 2010. At that time, WJ was driving the K&N-branded Pontiac GXP and Martino was crew chief for Northeast Pro Stock racer Bob Benza. (Photo Courtesy Auto Imagery)

to let me in. Arlene said sure, but Warren said, you can't give away any of our trade secrets. Then Mike Smith from their crew came over with a blanket to cover the motor, but instead he threw it over my head."

WJ was back to his brotherly ways, and from there the Knapps enjoyed a steady friendship with the Johnsons until Jon passed away in 2012. Joanne, who semi-retired from her motorsports career at the conclusion of the 2015 season, still speaks with the Johnsons and considers them both lifelong friends.

"Jon had a way with Warren that not everybody had," she said. "For some strange reason, they meshed. I'm going to say that was probably because Jon knew how to read Warren and when to bother him. They had a good relationship."

Getting the Quote (or Not)

National Dragster Editor Phil Burgess was hired to work for the sanctioning body's official publication before WJ had even earned his first win. Through the years, Burgess has reported on every category and gained insight into the racing and sometimes personal lives of innumerable drivers. He has seen the ebb and flow of the sport from the inside and is known for offering impartial, thoughtful, and thorough coverage. Well-respected in the drag racing community, Burgess has a knack for telling the truth in the very tricky position of reporting facts while being paid by the NHRA.

"I think one of the good things about WJ is that he will tell you what's on his mind, but that's also one of the bad things," said Burgess. "His opinion doesn't always jive with your own or what might be politically correct, but it is always enlightening. It didn't take much to get him going, especially after a glass of wine at the end of the day, and he could hold court on anything you wanted to talk about. You would get the unvarnished truth, and maybe you didn't get the quote you wanted, but you knew where he stood. It gave insight into one of the greatest minds in drag racing."

Legendary NHRA broadcaster Dave McClelland interviews WJ in his pit area in 1992.

A Journalist's Perspective

National Dragster, the official publication of the NHRA, offered in-depth coverage of Pro Stock from the very beginning of the class. John Jodauga's first taste of what would become Pro Stock came at the 1964 Winternationals, where the Southern California teen observed S/S Thunderbolts and A/FX Comets driven by racers such as Don Nicholson, Gas Ronda, Butch Leal, and Ronnie Sox.

Already well on his way to being a noted illustrator who would one day design striking press kits for Bill "Grumpy" Jenkins and historical art, including paintings celebrating KJ's 6-second pass and WJ's barrier-breaking 200-mph run, Jodauga was infused with inspiration.

The event set the course of his life, and Jodauga eventually became one of drag racing's most published illustrators, and later, a respected associate editor for *National Dragster*. Until retiring in 2013, his beat was Pro Stock.

"Warren Johnson was one of the guys that I really looked forward to interviewing," said Jodauga. "He gave me so much good information, but not only that, he was just very entertaining to talk to. He was so well versed on

By 2011, WJ's most victorious years as a driver were winding down. However, he was nowhere near finished with his career in engine development. (Photo Courtesy Auto Imagery)

so many subjects, and no matter how busy he was, he always took time to come over and talk to me. Technically speaking, he was a very good source of information. He knew everything there was to know about Pro Stock."

Among the moments that stand out for Jodauga in his time covering drag racing is the 1994 Pro Stock final in Houston. There, WJ and former teammate Scott Geoffrion put on that epic show in front of a cheering crowd with a tense starting-line burndown.

"That was around the time that the Wayne County Speed Shop scandal broke out; it was alleged that they were cheating," Jodauga remembered. "Warren and Kurt raced Darrell Alderman and Geoffrion in the final qualifying session, and they both lost. The Dodges were qualified No. 1 and No. 2, and it really looked like one of them would win the race. But on Sunday, WJ had to race Alderman in the semis, and he beat him. Then, in the final round, he had that really long burndown with Geoffrion and beat him. He beat both of them that day, and to me, that was Warren's finest hour. That's something you never forget.

"The funny thing about it, though, was that he never made a big deal about the scandal even though, if the Dodges really were using nitrous, he would have been cheated out of two or three championships. He was the one hurt the most by it, but he never made a big deal about it."

That may have been, at least in part, because of WJ's relationship off-track with Geoffrion. They were fierce competitors when they pulled to the starting line, but Scott had driven a second car for WJ before he was offered a seat in a factory-backed Dodge Pro Stocker, and they had spent time as friends even before that.

"When Scott died in 2006, it really hit Warren hard," said Jodauga. "I believe his exact words were that it 'shocked the s—— out of him."

WJ didn't sugarcoat anything, but one could count on the fact that his expressions were always truthful and never, ever boring.

Still Feisty

The 2005 season was designated as the end of an era for WJ when full-time sponsorship was just about to run dry. WJ had long said that he wasn't going to race on his own dime, so it was an easy decision to put retirement on the table when he learned that the financial side of things would be taking a turn at the end of the year. Drag racing was his job, and if he couldn't make money doing it, then it didn't make sense for him to continue.

WJ was never shy in his criticism of the sanctioning body's catering to the nitro cars, but that didn't halt Warren Johnson Racing from building friendships with some of the main players in the flopper and digger categories. The Oberhofer brothers, Jim O and Jon O, are seen here with "Big Dave" Cobert on the edge of WJ's pit area.

It was clearly evident, though, that despite his all-business exterior, WJ was still enjoying the ride. In Denver that season, he met up with young gun Dave Connolly in the final round. Connolly had made his Pro Stock debut in Chicago in 2003 with power supplied by Pro Stock legend Bill "Grumpy" Jenkins, who got his start in Pro Stock right around the time WJ did, in the dawning days of the class.

Connolly was young and had a reputation for being a little on the overly confident side, but he took his lumps in the early days like anyone else. KJ had walloped him in his first final round, and then it was Greg Anderson's turn. In each of Connolly's next three finals, Anderson was the winner, but the kid turned it around in Brainerd to claim his first win at Anderson's expense.

By the Pomona Winternationals in 2005, Connolly had three Pro Stock wins on his resume, and he made it a fourth with a final-round defeat of WJ, who was then all the way up to 94 trophies earned. Perhaps their previous rendezvous was on WJ's mind heading into the Denver final.

After defeating Erica Enders, Ron Krisher, and Jim Yates, WJ reached the closing round at Bandimere Speedway, a venue where he had been scooping up wins since 1984, the year after Connolly was born. On the other side of the ladder, the youngster had pocketed round wins over Mike Thomas, Anderson, and KJ to print a ticket to another battle with the Professor.

In each of the previous two rounds, Connolly had parlayed a better reaction time into a holeshot win. One would imagine that he was somewhat more confident than normal as he rolled forward from his burnout next to the Professor.

As the No. 2 qualifier, WJ knew he had a fast car and had been proving it all day. Connolly, starting from the No. 9 position, was aware that he needed to launch efficiently if he was going to have a fair chance at defeating the veteran in the race car beside him.

Both drivers lit the pre-stage bulbs, but then there was no forward movement from either side of the racetrack. WJ and Connolly sat idling for nearly 2 minutes, neither willing to stage first. The sold-out crowd rose to its feet with a raucous,

Veteran racer WJ and Pro Stock newcomer Erica Enders. The two never met in a final round, but in 2012, the Professor dealt the young lady one of six of her first-round losses that season. (Photo Courtesy Auto Imagery)

lengthy roar of approval until finally, WJ nudged the nose of his Pontiac in first.

The tree came down, and Connolly left the starting line 0.001 second too soon. His red light triggered the win light for WJ, who made his quickest run of the day, a 7.131-second pass paired with a top speed of 193.16 mph.

Jenkins had watched the entire ordeal play out from behind Connolly's car on the starting line with arms crossed. When the win light came on for WJ, the television camera panned to "Grumpy," who almost seemed to be grinning behind his characteristic cigar.

At the top end, when ESPN journalist Gary Gerould asked WJ if he had used "The School's Out Tour" to "school" Connolly, WJ said, "I don't know if I took him to school, but I taught that punk a lesson."

Later, in speaking with the media at Bandimere Speedway, WJ explained that he was aware that Connolly liked to stage last, so he packed his engine with ice to keep it cool and overfilled it with fuel in anticipation of a good, old-fashioned burndown.

He congratulated Connolly at the top end on an excellent day of driving, and the two went their separate ways, never again to meet in a final round.

"I did have some fun with it every once in a while," said WJ. "Geoffrion and Connolly and a few of those shenanigans that went on back in the day. But in reality, it was just part of the show. Having done so much match racing, I understood that you had to have some of that. If it's just two people going down the racetrack, and there isn't any emotion in it, it can get really bland. I'd like some fisticuffs or shouting every once in a while. The PC [politically correct] crap will kill everything."

CHAPTER 12

ACCOLADES AND ADVENTURE

Warren Johnson's career has rightfully been recognized and celebrated across a variety of publications and venues. It's a true testament to a career well spent when a racer begins to be inducted into respected halls of fame, and WJ has been an honored inductee in some very prestigious institutions.

International Motorsports Hall of Fame

His induction into the International Motorsports Hall of Fame on April 26, 2007, was particularly notable, as WJ was just the seventh member of the drag racing community to be included. Previous quarter-mile inductees into the International Motorsports Hall of Fame were Wally Parks, Bob Glidden, Don Garlits, Shirley Muldowney, Don Prudhomme, and Joe Amato.

Although qualifications to be nominated state that a person must be retired from his or her specialty in motorsports for at least five years, WJ was approved for induction based on the very special circumstance of having earned 96 NHRA wins to that point, along with 136 No.

KJ's children, Conner, Jarrett, and Erin, accompanied their grandfather to Talladega for his induction into the International Motorsports Hall of Fame.

WJ was inducted into the International Motorsports Hall of Fame in 2007. His old public relations team, Jon and Joanne Knapp, was also in attendance for the special event, which took place at Talladega Superspeedway.

The Professor's Way: Lesson 31

"When I look at motorsports in general, I still maintain that the reason anybody excels at it is because they love it," Warren Johnson said. "You put a lot more effort into something you love, and that's why you get the results. All we're talking about is a human body and part of a mechanical machine. It's a case of applying yourself and making the sacrifices. It's a simple formula that applies to any endeavor."

The Motorsports Hall of Fame of America inducted WJ in 2015. He was joined at the ceremony by his son, KJ, and his grandsons Conner and Jarrett.

Motorsports Hall of Fame of America

In 2015, WJ became the 16th drag racing personality in history to be inducted into the Motorsports Hall of Fame of America, joining a list of respected legends such as nitro pilots John Force and Kenny Bernstein, NHRA pioneers C. J. "Pappy" Hart and Wally Parks, and fellow Pro Stock campaigners Bill Jenkins and Bob Glidden.

The Motorsports Hall of Fame of America has been carefully selecting its honorees since 1989 through a process of voting by 200 racing experts, including historians, journalists, category experts, and previous inductees. The Hall of Fame of America's prestigious bronze Horsepower award was presented to WJ at its annual ceremony in Daytona Beach in March 2015.

NHRA's 50 Greatest Racers

Another well-deserved honor bestowed upon the Professor was his inclusion on the NHRA's list of 50 Greatest Racers. Johnson was No. 7 on the list, comprised in 2000 by a panel of experts as part of the following year's NHRA 50th anniversary celebration. *National Dragster* Editor Phil Burgess assembled the panel, which included historians, journalists, former racers, and officials.

The top 10 on the list spotlighted the best of the best, with Don Garlits in the No. 1 position, followed by John Force, Don Prudhomme, Bob Glidden, Shirley Muldowney, Kenny Bernstein, Warren Johnson, Bill Jenkins, Joe Amato, and Dale Armstrong.

1–qualifier awards, 830 round wins with a 0.681 winning percentage, 6 U.S. Nationals crowns, 149 final-round appearances, and having set low ET 139 times and top speed at 205 events. WJ's barrier-breaking 180-, 190-, and 200-mph passes, plus his 25 national speed records, tipped the scales in his favor for the 150-member voting panel comprised of American auto racing media.

The International Motorsports Hall of Fame was founded in 1990 by Bill France Jr., the son of the founder of NASCAR. Previous inductees included motorsports trailblazers such as Smokey Yunick, Al and Bobby Unser, Mickey Thompson, Carroll Shelby, Henry Ford, Jack Roush, Junior Johnson, and Parnelli Jones.

"It humbles you, to a certain extent," said WJ. "You look at the past recipients there, and even just being included in that conversation is an honor. There were a lot of people who had done a lot of great things."

The NHRA compiled a list of the 50 Greatest Racers of all time in celebration of its 50th anniversary in 2001. Johnson was No. 7 on the list for his six NHRA Pro Stock championships, multitude of national event wins, regular smashing of national records, and his groundbreaking advancements in technology. In 1999, he stood on the championship stage, honored with his fifth NHRA Pro Stock championship. From left to right are Matt Hines (Pro Stock Motorcycle), Tony Schumacher (Top Fuel), Bob Panella Jr. (Pro Stock Truck), Miss Winston Jackie Becke, SME President Rick Sanders, John Force (Funny Car), then-NHRA President Tom Compton, WJ, and Dallas Gardner. (Photo Courtesy Auto Imagery)

Division 2 Hall of Fame

WJ was also inducted into the NHRA's Division 2 Hall of Fame, alongside Southern Pro Stock Circuit founder Steve Earwood and Sportsman champion David Rampy. The Georgia Racing Hall of Fame inducted WJ in 2012 along with Daytona 500 champion Pete Hamilton, Dixie Speedway champ Bill Ingram, dirt track and asphalt racer Doug Kenimer, and sprint car champion Herman Wise.

Legends of Thunder Valley

In 2013, WJ was honored as one of Bristol Dragway's Legends of Thunder Valley. His name is enshrined atop the grandstands with only a handful of others, including Garlits, Force, and Schumacher. The Mesabi East Athletic Hall of Fame brought WJ home to Virginia, Minnesota, where he was inducted in 2016.

The Best of All Time?

"Not that long ago, I was asked who I considered the best Pro Stock driver of all time," said WJ. "That isn't an easy question to answer. Is Hank Aaron a better home run hitter than Babe Ruth? They come from two different eras. Babe Ruth was raised on pretzels and beer, and Hank Aaron had trainers and dieticians. He broke the record, but who is really the better home run hitter? That's something you can't answer. Every season, every circumstance is different.

"We're in an era now of drivers who have 15 people working on their cars. When Glidden and I were racing, the crew was three people: the driver, the wife, and the kid. It was a family operation. I would rather be known as a better racer than a driver. You build it, drive it to the track, and race it. This is a completely different era."

Six NHRA championships, two in the IHRA, and 97 national event wins have placed WJ at the top of the all-time list for many Pro Stock devotees. (Photo Courtesy Auto Imagery)

In 2015, WJ was honored to be inducted into the Mesabi East Athletic Hall of Fame in Aurora, Minnesota.

Around the World

It should come as no surprise that WJ is not particularly fond of taking time off. He has never been a fan of extended (or even brief) vacations, doesn't compre-

Having a major sponsor brought along marketing obligations that allowed WJ to establish a connection to the fans. WJ and his wife, Arlene, participated in many appearances for Oldsmobile and its ACDelco brand. "I don't recall that there were any real full-time sponsors then, for anyone. A lot of people had sponsorship through nepotism, but that doesn't count."

hend a desire to spend a week sipping cocktails on the beach during the "off-season," and never even considered the block of months between the last race of one season and the first race of the next a reason to take time off. In fact, WJ viewed the off-season as an opportunity to make further performance gains and work on projects that stimulated his mind.

However, when he was invited to travel to foreign destinations in support of the program, he was absolutely game. Sponsor GM Performance twice hosted WJ and crew on the Caribbean island of Puerto Rico to be part of special exhibition races. The events were put on for sales representatives from ACDelco's network of global authorized auto parts distributors.

Getting there posed something of a logistical issue. The first time they were asked to race in Puerto Rico, they were given a short time period to put all the pieces in place. They were able to ship the race car, but the tractor trailer in which it normally traveled wasn't invited. The roads simply weren't wide enough to accommodate the setup, and so they borrowed a tagalong trailer from a private party to use during the whirlwind trip.

"They have a real car culture down there," said WJ. "As small as the island is, it had two drag strips. They're all basically gearheads down there, so it was pretty well

The ACDelco family invited WJ to Puerto Rico to partake in exhibition races twice. There, he became good friends with the crew. Angel Ramos sits in the driver's seat of WJ's Oldsmobile Cutlass. (Photo Courtesy Carlos Ivan Gonzalez)

WJ poses for a photo with his crew at the ACDelco race in Puerto Rico. "It didn't matter where we were or what the event was, anytime I raced, the object was to win," said WJ. "I didn't care who was in the other lane. I didn't care if it was God, I'd still want to beat him. We had an enjoyable time there in Puerto Rico. It was a pretty nice track and a really nice facility, even compared to some of the tracks we race on here." (Photo Courtesy Carlos Ivan Gonzalez)

but when rain delayed the Winston Finals, the weekends were suddenly in competition.

Scott Geoffrion, who was driving the second Olds Cutlass for WJ that year, was on the roster for Japan, but with the sudden scheduling conflict WJ surmised it would be better for Geoffrion to stay behind and complete the season. WJ could finish no better than second place to Darrell Alderman, and Geoffrion was still in the hunt for his first win after reaching two finals that year and had the opportunity to move up in the points.

So, WJ went off to Japan to join friend and fellow Pro Stock racer Harry Scribner, among others. They raced against turbocharged V-6 and straight-six combinations piloted by Japanese racers from the Roadrunner Racing Club.

The drag strip was on the straightaway of the road course, and to protect the racing surface, competitors were only allowed to perform a burnout on a specially designated pad located just off the track. They would then drive up to the starting line to stage and make a pass.

WJ was particularly fast with his ACDelco-branded Cutlass and, ultimately, won the event. As noted in a

received. I would say it was a positive experience for everybody, including us."

WJ took his program international in 1991 to participate in the USA Drag Festival in Gotemba, Japan, at Fuji International Speedway. The event had been scheduled to take place after the NHRA season had concluded,

The ACDelco Olds Cutlass is at a drag strip on the Caribbean island of Puerto Rico. (Photo Courtesy Carlos Ivan Gonzalez)

late-season issue of *National Dragster* in 1991, his Olds outran the Willie Rells–built Blitz Escort 300ZX driven by Akhito Ukon, 7.67 to 8.95, in the first round, and WJ beat Scribner in the final, 7.54 to 7.71.

"They had a helluva crowd," said WJ, who was pleased to have the fastest car by a longshot. "There had to easily be 40,000 people there. That was a really interesting experience, and I think we were there 10 days. We got a pretty good tour of Japan, rode the first bullet train they had there, stayed at Lake Yamanaka, which wasn't far from Mount Fuji and where the speedway was. I enjoyed it. It was something different."

The most impactful events that WJ participated in were the USO-sponsored goodwill trips to visit wounded American troops and Air Force/Army personnel.

WJ traveled the globe throughout his career. (Photo Courtesy Auto Imagery)

Simmonds Says

The partnership that Warren Johnson shared with General Motors was one of the longest and strongest in the history of the sport. More than two decades of collaboration produced a plethora of victories both on and off the track as WJ's success surged along with GM's recognition as a capable and powerful automotive brand.

Fred Simmonds spent countless hours with WJ over the years, first as the Pontiac Motorsports marketing manager and then as the GM Racing Group drag racing manager. Simmonds was along on many of the USO goodwill tours with WJ, and they frequently engaged in conversation both at and away from the racetrack. Well-known and respected in the drag racing community, and especially in Pro Stock, Simmonds shared WJ's dedication to his chosen craft.

"I can't think of any driver who's had a more important impact on his class," said Simmonds in 2005. "From a performance standpoint and even from a safety standpoint. When you think of General Motors and drag racing, one name comes to mind: 'the Professor,' Warren Johnson."

WJ is with Fred Simmonds from GM Racing Group in 2002. (Photo Courtesy Auto Imagery)

Johnson in Japan

"It struck me how clean that town was," Warren Johnson said. "I'm not much for sleeping, so I'd walk downtown Tokyo at two or three in the morning. There were smoke and curio shops around town, and they'd close up at night and just turn the lights off but leave everything out. I asked one of the traffic cops—they were at every intersection—about it one night and he said they didn't allow crime. You could take a briefcase full of hundred-dollar bills with money sticking out of the corners, put it in the middle of the five-way intersection, and it would still be there next year. I don't know if it's the same nowadays, but at that point in time, I felt totally comfortable there and very welcomed. It was certainly a pleasant experience."

WJ was coined an "International Champion" after racing in Japan for the USA Drag Festival. The event took place in Gotemba at Fuji International Speedway. WJ beat Harry Scribner in the final round. (Photo Courtesy Auto Imagery)

WJ, Jason Line, Cory McClenathan, and Jim Yates pose for a photo with navy personnel aboard a gunship in 2007. WJ was a regular on the GM-sponsored NHRA USO Tour. (Publicity Photo Courtesy GM)

On the USO tour at Kuwait's Camp Arifjan in 2007. From left to right are GM's Jeff Romack and NHRA drivers Jim Yates, Jason Line, Cory McLanathan, WJ, and GM's Fred Simmonds.

He joined the annual tour with fellow GM Performance drivers during the offseason in 2005. They traveled to the Kaiserslautern Military Community in Frankfurt, Germany, and in later years incorporated stops in the Middle East to meet with men and women of the armed forces and bring them what they all hoped would be a meaningful boost of morale.

"It's probably one of the most satisfying things I've done in my career," said WJ. "For us as a group, to go over there and give a little back in return for the immense sacrifices that all of them have made, I mean, it was definitely more of an opportunity than a request to just do something. It was something all of us, collectively, felt we really needed to do."

Commercial Success

Representing a major sponsor comes with inherent responsibility, and not all of it is based on winning races. For many contracted athletes and personalities, there is a level of dread when it comes to fulfilling marketing obligations. But WJ's intense nature belied a playful side that only friends and close colleagues were usually privy to. Requests for participation in marketing and advertising events allowed the public to get a glimpse of the surprisingly jovial side to the Professor.

A new line of GM Goodwrench Service Tools was to be promoted on the QVC home shopping network just before the Route 66 Nationals in Chicago, and WJ was tapped as a guest on the Father's Day–themed show. There was no rehearsal, and the show was broadcast live from the studio.

"It was total chaos on the set," reported WJ, who shared the GM Goodwrench sponsorship with NASCAR's Dale Earnhardt and occasionally crossed paths with him at marketing events. "The host didn't know a ratchet from

WJ gets "ticketed" by an Elbert County sheriff at a marketing event.

WJ hosted the Elbert County Sheriff's Department at the Sugar Hill, Georgia, race shop. The officers had the opportunity to check out the inside of a 200-plus-mph Pro Stock car.

The Professor's Way: Lesson 32

"Bob Glidden was unknown at one time, and so was Bill Jenkins," Warren Johnson said. "They weren't overnight successes, and neither was I. The cliché that says you have to pay your dues really means you have to become educated. You have to assess all the factors, look at your strengths and weaknesses, and build a program that's competitive."

WJ in the winner's circle at Dallas in 1999, having a chat with Bill "Grumpy" Jenkins. That's GM representative Fred Simmonds on the far right. (Photo Courtesy Auto Imagery)

NHRA's Lewis Bloom interviews WJ in the winner's circle after the 2001 victory in St. Louis. (Photo Courtesy Auto Imagery)

a jack handle, but it was pretty hilarious from my standpoint. I had a good time, and I think we sold a few tools."

GM Goodwrench tools were also at the center of a television commercial for K-Mart, a national chain of retail big-box stores. The spot was filmed at the Sugar Hill, Georgia, race shop and featured both WJ and his wife, Arlene. WJ used the brand's swivel-head ratchet as he wrenched away on one of his Pro Stock engines.

No Salt for WJ

One venture that was publicized in its infancy but did not come to fruition was WJ's involvement in a project in 2018 that would have brought him to the Bonneville Salt Flats. He was approached by an individual who had a relatively small displacement engine that he wished to push past the 370-mph marker in a streamliner. Having never been to the annual August event, it triggered WJ's interest.

Noting that the existing naturally aspirated 260-ci engine was very much "an antique," the Professor realized that a significant amount of work was required. An up-to-date engine would have to be built, and it would need to be modified to a compact product to fit the application. WJ was confident that he could accomplish the task and began to enlist the assistance of fellow engine expert Richard Maskin to create some of the necessary parts.

"It could easily have produced power at the level needed, but they don't race for money out there—they race for hats," said WJ. "I can get a hat at the Goodwill. I don't do this for free, and when I explained what the engine would cost, we came to realize that it wasn't something that they were in a financial position to pursue. If they come up with the wherewithal to complete the project and achieve what they want to achieve later in time, I would consider being part of it. In the meantime, I'm happy to give them tips on stuff they're working on."

The Goodwrench Service Plus Pontiac Grand Am. (Photo Courtesy Auto Imagery)

CHAPTER 13

POSTGRAD

In the year 2000, Warren Johnson stated for the record that his program was focused on long-term research and development, and that has proven to be true. Two decades later, he is still just as dedicated to his craft, and he is still sought after for his expertise.

The last season of the Pontiac Firebird for WJ was 2000, and the car was dressed in a silver anniversary paint scheme. Ahead of the season, WJ reflected, "As the saying goes, the longest journey starts with a single step. We slept in the truck and took showers in our friends' hotel rooms at the races, but at least we brought our own towels," he joked. "We just didn't have any sponsorship money or anything to fall back on in 1975. I had no choice but to make it work." (Photo Courtesy Auto Imagery)

The 2005 School's Out Tour was meant to mark the end of an era, and in its own way, it did. GM Performance Parts was planning to shift gears at the conclusion of the

The GM Performance Parts Chevrolet that WJ drove in 2005 was branded with "The School's Out Tour" across the front end. The year was touted as his final behind the wheel, but he arrived back at the racetrack with renewed financial support in 2006. (Photo Courtesy Auto Imagery)

A much-delayed Maple Grove Raceway winner's circle took place under cloudy skies in 2003. WJ (far right) was victorious along with (from left to right) Michael Phillips (Pro Stock Motorcycle), Tim Wilkerson (Funny Car), and Tony Schumacher (Top Fuel). (Photo Courtesy Auto Imagery)

Never bashful about voicing his opinion, WJ was sometimes tricky to represent in terms of public relations, but part of what made the Professor so successful was that he pushed all the right boundaries. (Photo Courtesy Auto Imagery)

You never knew what you were going to get when interviewing WJ, but he always kept it interesting. Here, he stands with NHRA announcer Bob Frey in 2005 on a Sunday morning during prerace ceremonies. WJ brought the total package to the track every time he showed up—from his often-wry sense of humor to having a fully prepared race car capable of winning. "Warren had some truly epic seasons," said former PR representative Rick Voegelin. "You don't win as many championships or races in a season as he did by just showing up." (Photo Courtesy Auto Imagery)

season, and WJ made the most of what was slated to be the final races of his driving career.

But three wins in five final rounds equated to a top-10 finish for the 26th time in his career. He was No. 4 in the

WJ and his crew (from left to right: Mike Smith, Dain Schwan, WJ, and Adam Drzayich) celebrate in 2006. All three of these former crewmembers went on to use the knowledge that they gathered under WJ's tutelage to advance their careers in positive ways. Smith brought his engine-building expertise to other Pro Stock teams, Schwann crafted a career as a machinist, and Drzayich launched a service geared toward helping Sportsman racers run a more efficient program. (Photo Courtesy Auto Imagery)

standings at the sound of the final buzzer, and school was back in session for Johnson and his GM Performance Parts Pontiac GTO at the 2006 Winternationals.

As long as the funding was there, WJ would race, and he said that as far as he was concerned, retirement involved a pine box.

The 2006 season brought along another monster milestone, his 500th career race, another first in NHRA history. The year was highlighted by a win in Phoenix over Greg Anderson. WJ finished eighth in the nation the following year and was runner-up to Anderson in Atlanta, but three more years would pass before he was back in the winner's circle.

It happened on a very strange day in 2010. WJ was behind the wheel of his K&N Filters–branded Pontiac GXP at the St. Louis–area racing facility that served as host of the NHRA Midwest Nationals. Qualified in the No. 12 spot, WJ drew No. 5 qualifier Ron Krisher in the first round of eliminations. WJ dropped a holeshot on his opponent with a not-exactly stellar 0.069-second

One of WJ's most worthy opponents proved to be his son. KJ and WJ met in the final round 13 times, and in 1993 KJ finished No. 2 in the nation to his father. (Photo Courtesy Auto Imagery)

"I didn't work in somebody's shop. I had to learn it. That's the difference," said WJ. (Photo Courtesy Auto Imagery)

The last major sponsorship for WJ was in 2010 when he flew the colors of K&N Filters on his Pontiac GXP. "These cars will continue to go quicker and faster as long as people continue to work on them, work on them correctly, and keep utilizing better and better materials," said WJ. "You just keep working on it. It borders on insanity." (Photo Courtesy Auto Imagery)

WJ talks shop with Mike Edwards in the staging lanes at Houston in 2010. Edwards came on strong in 2009 to earn his first Pro Stock championship. Edwards and WJ met in the final round four times, and WJ came up a winner on three of those occasions. (Photo Courtesy Auto Imagery)

The victory in 2010 at the NHRA Midwest Nationals moved WJ up to 97 Pro Stock wins, a massive number that no other driver in the category had yet to touch by the time this book went to print in 2020. (Photo Courtesy Brandon Mudd)

Every one of both WJ and KJ's crew were on the starting line, and they celebrated raucously when the win light came on in the Professor's lane on a very unusual day at Gateway Motorsports Park near St. Louis. WJ scored strange and lucky wins as one opponent after the other ran into mysterious maladies. In the final, Jeg Coughlin Jr.'s stumble was WJ's victory. (Photo Courtesy Auto Imagery)

Just as it was in the beginning, WJ never had a large crew. For his 2010 victory at St. Louis, it was just WJ, Adam Drzayich (left), and Randy Chambers. (Photo Courtesy Auto Imagery)

reaction time to a sleepy 0.114 and buffed it into a shiny new round win with a slower but victorious 6.685 at 207.08 mph to a 6.666 at 206.86 mph.

When No. 4 qualifier Allen Johnson had troubles with the racetrack in round two, WJ surged ahead on a 6.692 at 207.11 mph and scored a semifinals meeting with No. 1–qualifier Mike Edwards. When defending world champ Edwards couldn't get his car to fire, WJ scored a freebie and wheeled his way to a 6.668 at 207.56 mph.

Riding a wave of good fortune, WJ was headed to the final round for the first time since the Atlanta race in 2007. He forfeited lane choice to Jeg Coughlin for their final-round meeting. Coughlin had just laid down a stunning pass in the semifinals, a 6.607 at 208.17 mph that was low ET of the meet, but that proved to be inconsequential.

When Coughlin dropped the clutch, his Pro Stocker shuddered and then shut off. He rolled slowly through the beams and watched as the Professor scooped up his lucky win.

On the starting line, the small crew, consisting of just Adam Drzayich and Randy Chambers, plus KJ, and KJ's crew, went wild. They matched the excitement of the crowd at what was then known as Gateway Motorsports Park. It had been 98 races since WJ's last win.

WJ was 62 years old when he won Phoenix in 2006 over Anderson. He was the oldest professional NHRA winner then and the oldest again when he won that day in St. Louis at the age of 66. At that time, the list of winners over the age of 60 was short: WJ (66), John Force (60), Ron Krisher (61), V. Gaines (60), and Eddie Hill (60).

On the starting line in utter disbelief, KJ said it all boiled down to teamwork, determination, and a lot of luck. At the top end, WJ was smiling as big as ever as he extracted himself from his race car.

"You keep working at it and working at it, because really, this is all we do for a living," WJ told ESPN's Gary Gerould. "We just keep beating and banging on these things, and sooner or later . . . We haven't turned a corner yet. We can see it, but we don't know which direction it's going."

That day in St. Louis was a mile marker of sorts. WJ's driving career began to wind down after that, tapering off year by year until 2014, when he raced at just one event: the Southern Nationals in Atlanta. At his last race on record, WJ beat Dave Connolly in the first round before Greg Anderson sent him home in round two.

The Atlanta event was his 649th NHRA national event, leaving him just one shy of what seems like a better stopping point, 650. Even more aggravating, to those who like numbers and statistics, is that WJ is just three wins short of 100. There are other drivers who have crossed that threshold, but no one had done it yet in Pro Stock when WJ parked his car after the Atlanta race, and it still hadn't been done when this book went to print.

That didn't sit well with a lot of people, particularly WJ fans who could see Greg Anderson, who was something of a nemesis in their eyes, coming up from behind. For WJ, though, it was just a number.

"I've been very fortunate to win as many races as I have, but someone will surpass what I've done someday," he said. "That's just reality. I don't think about any of the records or numbers. I don't have a huge ego. I may be a little more intense than most people, but I just enjoy what I do. I don't think about records. That's not why I'm in this business."

Warren Johnson's 97 Wins by Track	
Track	Wins
Pomona, California	10*
Gainesville, Florida	9**
Indianapolis, Indiana	6
Houston, Texas	6*
Atlanta, Georgia	5*
Dallas, Texas	5
Denver, Colorado	5
Topeka, Kansas	5*
Brainerd, Minnesota	4
Columbus, Ohio	4
Englishtown, New Jersey	4
Memphis, Tennessee	4
Reading, Pennsylvania	4
Richmond, Virginia	4
Seattle, Washington	4
Phoenix, Arizona	3
Sonoma, California	3
St. Louis, Missouri	3
Baton Rouge, Louisiana	2
Bristol, Tennessee	2
Chicago, Illinois	2
Fremont, California	1
Irvine, California	1
Montreal, Canada	1

* More wins at the facility than any other Pro Stock driver.
** More wins at the facility than any driver in any professional category.

The Crew

WJ said that he had many great employees over the years and that they were valuable contributors to the success of Warren Johnson Enterprises (WJE).

"We all worked so hard to win those races," he said. "We knew when we showed up that we had the ability to win. That doesn't guarantee it, but we knew we were prepared. I was supposed to be the leader of the group, so when things didn't go right, I could only look at myself."

Many of the individuals whom WJ hired stayed quite a while, and there is an impressively long list of people who passed through the doors of WJE during four decades of successful racing. Many of them went on to great careers in the industry, a fact that WJ said he finds rewarding.

WJ enjoyed conversation on a variety of subjects when the timing was appropriate. Here he is spending a few moments with friend Doug Bang between qualifying rounds at Brainerd International Raceway in 1988.

Pat Barrett

Among those with perhaps the longest tenure was fellow Minnesotan Pat Barrett. He worked with the team off and on for quite a few years during their decades-long friendship, which began in 1967. Barrett once raced a Super Stock AMC powered by a WJ engine and later had the honor of contributing to many of WJ's Pro Stock victories. Barrett, a computer and electronics specialist, moved from Minnesota to Georgia, not far from WJ's shop, after retirement.

The three amigos of Warren Johnson Racing in the 1990s: Ray Prince, Buzzy Woitas, and Pat Barrett at the Dallas race in 1991.

Robert "Gordie" Gordon and Ray Prince

Another longtime employee and friend was Robert "Gordie" Gordon, a former Pennsylvania highway patrolman who drove the team's transporter and was with the team from 1989 until 1997.

Truck driver and mechanic Ray Prince first met WJ in 1985; he brought firsthand racing knowledge to the team from campaigning a Stock Eliminator Mustang in the 1970s.

Notable WJE employees

Former competitor Buddy Ingersoll was on the payroll for half a year at one point. Pro Stock veteran Terry Adams made a brief stop in the WJE camp for 2007 before moving on to being the crew chief for Mike

Testing on a Monday at Brainerd International Raceway set a different tone than what was felt on race weekends. WJ and good friends Pat and Kathy Barrett have a laugh in the staging lanes in 1990 ahead of a pass.

KJ and Arlene are pictured with Bruce "Bill Bailey" Dailey and Robert "Gordie" Gordon in the mid-1990s.

Longtime crewmember Robert "Gordie" Gordon works on the Olds Cutlass between rounds.

WJ (center) with Robert "Gordie" Gordon (left) at Pomona's Auto Club Raceway in 1992.

Edwards during his 2009 championship season. Motorsports veteran Jeff Perley was with the team from 1997 until 2001, when Greg Anderson put together the KB Racing Pro Stock team and invited him on board. Clutch and transmission specialist Mike Stryker won the Parts America Mechanic of the Year award by a landslide for the team in 1998 and later worked with a number of Pro Stock teams, including those led by Greg Stanfield and Chris McGaha.

The Final Crew

Mike Smith, who moved on to work in engine development for Pro Stock's Gray Motorsports, Adam Drzayich, and Randy Chambers worked with WJ in his final few seasons as a driver.

Drzayich, who grew up in drag racing and has campaigned cars of his own, launched a business of his own after the team disbanded. He provides professional services to Sportsman drag racers, including racetrack tuning and data acquisition.

"You couldn't ask for a better guy to work for," said Drzayich. "He's reasonable, patient, and will teach you anything you want to know. If you screw something up once, he'll stand there and laugh at you—but he'll tell you, let's try this again. He doesn't get upset. He expects a lot, but that's a given when you work for someone with his credentials in this sport."

Powered by WJ

WJ's reputation as a record breaker, power maker, and dominator has made his expertise a hot commodity. Although he has never been

Bill Smith perched inside of KJ's Pro Stocker as it is prepared for a race. Get a load of that shifter.

keen on making a business of leasing engines, there has been a tidy list of racers whom he has assisted, dating all the way back to 1969. That was the year Herb Lang won the A/SA class at the U.S. Nationals with WJ power out of his Competition Engine Service Inc. shop in Fridley, Minnesota.

A Comp Title for Ellis

The NHRA's 2013 Lucas Oil Drag Racing Series Competition Eliminator world champion, Alan Ellis, scored his first series title in his 1923 roadster using power supplied by WJE. His success proved the longevity of WJ's DRCE-2, which WJ had last raced in 1996. They were engines that WJ had "parked in a corner," and Ellis bought one, saw how fast it was, and came back to buy the other.

Carbery's National Record

There was no shortage of work at WJE headquarters in the late 2000s, so it took some convincing from KJ to get WJ to agree to supply engines to Comp racer Pete Carbery. The Odessa-based Comp racer had tried his hand at Pro Stock in 2004, so he wasn't a stranger to the Johnson clan. After some thought, WJ was on board. It was a productive partnership in 2010 when Carbery piloted his B/A Chevrolet Cobalt to a 6.92-second pass at 200.50 mph that broke the national record.

In the Pro Stock ranks, Matt Hartford sought WJ power for the 2016 season, the first year of EFI for the class. Hartford explained, "There is no ego involved with him; he's just here to make the car and our team faster."

Although WJ could undoubtedly fire up a leasing program and generate a healthy wave of cash flow, he is just not interested.

"I like doing engine development and work at the shop, but I'm too old and crotchety to be a babysitter," he said.

That stance might hit a little painfully when the expanse of Warren Johnson Enterprises is taken into consideration. WJ's bottomless well of knowledge and ample machinery are complemented by a warehouse full of parts. Because he has never thrown anything away, there are rows and rows of pieces he has been accumulating for nearly 45 years: engine blocks, camshafts, manifolds, headers, nuts, bolts, and the list goes on and on. It's part warehouse, part museum.

"Once in a while I will go up there," WJ said, "usually when I'm going to get a particular part or something, and I'll look at things. It makes you think about the progression that we've made in developing this stuff. You start off at one point, and if you know where you want to go, hopefully you get there. Everything up there is proof of that."

State of Affairs

When WJ secured his first corporate sponsorship with Oldsmobile in 1983, it opened the door to a whole new world. It was a launching point that allowed him to build an empire. The financial stability from the partnership with General Motors gave WJ the means to invest in equipment and become self-sufficient, bringing as much of the work as possible in-house for a faster turnaround and better control over quality.

Money opened doors, but it wasn't the key to his success. WJ was willing to invest vast amounts of time, a resource seldom used to its fullest potential. He believed that the only way to make a business successful was to work at it, and that is what he did from the beginning, seven days a week. While others were racing for fun, WJ was toiling away, devoid of envy and solely focused on one task at a time toward the goal he intended to reach.

It could easily be argued that WJ simply outworked his competitors, and he did so at a steady, uniform pace, never falling into a frenzy. Once a project began, he stubbornly and methodically worked his way through it. Two things could derail a mission: lack of financial viability or the determination that the original goal was faulty and no longer worth striving for.

Because WJ was not concerned with what his competitors were doing and didn't take much of anything personally, he was able to evaluate the bigger picture even as he was part of it. Throughout his career and, really, his life, this allowed him to automatically and unemotionally see potential solutions to many problems.

As for the future of drag racing, WJ believes that there is still room and need for gasoline, alcohol, and nitro categories, and that one single category could not sustain the unique sport.

"The answer is in delving into the psyche of the spectators to really understand what interests them," he said. "We've accepted that this is the entertainment industry, and it's not just about racing your hot rod for self-gratification. There is a diverse crowd out there, and it's up to the sanctioning body to satisfy them."

While horsepower is still part of the equation, the new winning formula is an expensive cocktail. One must have the most efficient and effective block, suspension, shocks, springs, transmission, rear end, and timers—plus the complementing accoutrements for each—and then find a way to transfer the horsepower to the racetrack.

In addition to the ever-increasing mechanical challenge, the drivers themselves have shifted shape. WJ noted that there has been a decrease in duration as young drivers of wealth are typically "here today, gone tomorrow" players. He attributes the prominence of big money, short-term racing to the fact that there is no longer an evident path to racing for a living.

"We have a problem, and it can be solved," said WJ. "In order to fix what's gone wrong, we need an organized sanctioning body that is willing to acknowledge when the desired results aren't being achieved and make changes. What you need is a promoter, not a bean counter."

He also noted that there is a bushel of missed opportunity within the inner workings of today's teams. From the early days, the Pro Stock category has been identified as a class of secrecy. The team with the best research and development is the team with the best results, and effective research and development becomes a collection of classified information.

But no team has the same personnel for the duration of its existence, and a human being cannot unknow what he or she knows. Thus, information has gone from team to team in the Pro Stock pits with very few new thought processes involved.

"They have a very efficient package, but it's taken them years to get there," said WJ. "They know what they have, and they've been picking at it here and there, so they don't want anything new. I see that as a missed opportunity."

Still Humming

The expansive WJE shop is an engine builder's and a machinist's dream. The equipment isn't new, but it is well-cared for and does any job as efficiently as WJ demands.

All of the machining is done in-house, so blocks are received raw with only main caps bolted in place, and cylinder heads come in as raw castings. WJ wields his welding torch to build fixtures that will accommodate the necessary procedures. He and KJ are continuously updating their hands-on education with the CNC machine to build and run new

In 2003, WJ was racing and wrenching on a Pontiac Grand Am. The bright yellow scheme first made its debut in 2002, replacing the silver and black that had previously been favored. (Photo Courtesy Auto Imagery)

programs to bring to life designs that only the Professor could dream up.

The two share the heavy lifting with KJ managing much of the assembly and actively running the dyno. The dyno room is KJ's domain. It is an extension of the office, loaded with binders of notes and all types of memorabilia collected over two decades of well-decorated drag racing.

If WJ had chosen to sell or set aflame his fire suit and driving gloves at any point hereafter, not a single soul would blame him, but they're still in his closet, and his race helmet is sitting on the roof of his Pro Stock car in his shop in Sugar Hill, Georgia.

WJ admits that he has never missed driving. He has said that he enjoyed it if he had an ill-handling car because then it was more interesting, but for the most part, driving was just something that came with the territory. It was a way to test what he'd been working on in the shop, where he was really at home. He joked that in the beginning he only drove because Arlene wouldn't, KJ was too young, and the dog couldn't get a license.

Arlene and Warren Johnson began racing together as a family, fully committing in 1975. They are still heading into the race shop every day 45 years later.

Still, one may ponder what it would take to get WJ to step foot in a Pro Stock car again. In a 2015 interview with Joe Castello for WFO Radio, WJ answered the question.

"Well, we would have to have enough sponsor support to be competitive," said WJ, who has repeatedly said that he would not race on his own dime. "I don't want to go out there just to go out there. If I came back, it would be to whip everybody's ass."

In the meantime, the Professor is perfectly content to spend 12 to 14 hours in the shop seven days a week, working on whatever comes his way and digging into anything that piques his interest. When asked what he's up to, WJ—like always before—isn't apt to divulge many details.

WJ has not kept secret the fact that he has continued to work with Chevrolet's LS-based V-8 engines, which falls right in line with history. He was integral in the design of the GM Performance Parts LSX block in 2007, constructed to withstand racing stressors with no compromise in strength or limitations regarding compatibility with racing parts.

In one of the final interviews for this book, it took a bit longer than normal for WJ to pick up the phone. Arlene explained that he was under the car "doing who knows what." When he came on the line, WJ explained

that Pro Stock cars hadn't changed in 50 years, so he was in the midst of an exercise in engineering.

"Everybody has the same car, no matter who built it," he said. "If everyone has the same car, the same motors, and the same pieces, doesn't that mean they'll all go just as fast? So, let's reengineer the cars to be more efficient.

"When we were racing full time, we didn't have time to think about changing anything; we just tried to adapt to the characteristics of what the chassis were. Now, we've got pretty sophisticated shock-absorber technology, and that tells me that the chassis needs to be changed. So, I've got my welder and cutting torch out."

Even at 77 years of age, the Professor never rests. He rises early, heads to the shop in the 7 o'clock hour, pours a cup of coffee, and gets right to work. Throughout the day, the humming melody of various machines rise and fall. It is a background noise that Arlene, in the front office, doesn't seem to notice. She stays busy as well, answering phones that still seem to ring more often than not and venturing back to sweep up metal shavings or packing material when the machines go silent for a spell.

The Professor's Way: Lesson 33

"First, establish the goal," Warren Johnson said. "Once you understand the parameters, then you go to work. But you have to keep an open mind, because every day you learn something new."

Where Did "the Professor" Come From?

It's easy to understand why he came to be known as the Professor, but it's a little more difficult to nail down when WJ was christened with the nickname and who said it first. In a 2004 interview with the NHRA, WJ revealed his thoughts on the matter.

"I think it was John Brasseaux, a staff writer from *National Dragster*," WJ said. "He hung that moniker on me because I was so intense at what I was doing. He made the observation that, for me, it was more of an analytical approach to racing. I wasn't just throwing parts at a hot rod."

WJ celebrates the Brainerd win with fellow Minnesotan and family friend Jack Mattonen in 1995. (Photo Courtesy Auto Imagery)

It is a life of simple and consistent routine within which WJ's insatiable need for research and development is well fed. On any given day, you'll likely find him in worn black jeans and a faded black sweatshirt with the sleeves pushed up, using his mind and his hands to further his own education.

A big smile from the Professor in 2009. (Photo Courtesy Auto Imagery)

He does not look like the most prolific Pro Stock drag racer on the planet, an eight-time champion across two respected series with more trophies than can fit in the attic. He just looks like a normal guy, hard at work and happy to be there.

"Oh, I don't think I've done anything extraordinary," said Warren Johnson with a characteristic shrug. "I was just fortunate enough to race a car and make a living doing something I enjoy."

Class Dismissed.

The Professor's Way: Lesson 34

"The way I look at it, if I had a positive impact on anybody who was indecisive or unsure whether they had the ability or ambition to accomplish something, if I've helped anyone get over that hurdle, then I've had success," Warren Johnson said.

Grandson Conner sits in the driver's seat of WJ's Pro Stocker. None of the grandkids were bitten by the racing bug, but they don't know a life without drag racing.

WJ celebrates in the Atlanta winner's circle with his grandson Conner in 2013. (Photo Courtesy Auto Imagery)

NHRA announcer and host of WFO Radio, Joe Castello, interviews WJ in 2013. Anytime WJ attended a race after he stepped back from full-time racing, he would make his way to the starting line to watch the sport to which he dedicated his entire career. (Photo Courtesy Auto Imagery)

Jarrett, Erin, and Conner Johnson, KJ and Kathy's children, pose in 2020 at Erin's nursing school graduation party.

The NHRA holds WJ in high regard as one of the legends of the sport. In later years, he has been invited to national events for guest appearances and special exhibition races. In 2019, he signed autographs at the Mello Yello Powerhouse display in Atlanta with "Big Daddy" Don Garlits and current NHRA competitors Jerry Savoie (Pro Stock Motorcycle), Cruz Pedregon (Funny Car), Erica Enders (Pro Stock), and Doug Kalitta (Top Fuel).

In 2019, the NHRA put together a special exhibition at the Gatornationals in Gainesville to celebrate the 50th anniversary of the event. The exhibition shoot-out race featured legends of the sport going head to head in Toyota Camry street cars. (Toyota was the official car and truck of the NHRA at the time.) Although the cars were all the same make, model, and year, each was wrapped in a retro design recognizing the former rides of the respective drivers. WJ was significantly faster than his competitors, despite the even playing field. "They were all in it to win, the only problem is they only drove during their career; they never worked on a car," said WJ. "I was there to win the damn race." (Photo Courtesy Auto Imagery)

KJ and WJ are on the starting line in Columbus in 2001. They worked diligently together to claim 6 NHRA world championships, 97 national event wins for WJ, and 40 of those shiny Wally trophies for KJ.

WJ and KJ displayed unique Kidz Toyz wraps at the Las Vegas spring event in 2012. (Photo Courtesy Auto Imagery)

Captured in a 2019 photo, WJ still looks right at home on the starting line during Pro Stock, more than four decades after going all-in. (Photo Courtesy Auto Imagery)

At the Atlanta race in 2011, WJ brought out his Chevrolet Cobalt with a nostalgic look honoring the car he referred to as "Butterbean." The deep red 2011 Chevy had the familiar silver WJ logo on the door, mirroring the paint scheme he had on his 1981 Oldsmobile Starfire. (Photo Courtesy Auto Imagery)

The Professor in 2000. (Photo Courtesy Auto Imagery)

WARREN JOHNSON'S LASTING LEGACY

Championship Breakdown					
Year	Wins	Total Races	Final Rounds	No. 1–Qualifier Awards	Points (Amount by which Season Was Won)
1992	8	18	9	4	3,222
1993	9	18	12	14	3,506
1995	7	19	9	14	305*
1998	9	22	12	13	440
1999	7	22	9	15	344
2001	6	24	6	3	79

*New NHRA points system began; round wins previously worth 200 marks now worth 20.

Hits of the 1990s	
Year	Details
1990	Sets national record for speed at Dallas (192.18 mph); runner-up in Pro Stock bonus event; six No. 1–qualifier awards; one win in three final rounds
1991	Sets national record for ET at Reading (7.180 seconds); 5 wins in 11 final rounds; No. 1 at eight events; crowned International Pro Stock champion (more on this in chapter 12)
1992	Wins first NHRA Pro Stock championship; national records for speed at Houston (193.38 mph), Gainesville (194.46), Sonoma (194.51); eight victories in nine final rounds; No. 1 four times in qualifying
1993	Wins second NHRA Pro Stock championship; sets national records for ET and speed at Houston (7.027, 195.05), speed at Gainesville (196.24); 9 wins in 12 final rounds; led Pro Stock points for entire season; 14 No.-1 qualifier awards; wins first Pro Stock bonus race
1994	WJ horsepower sends KJ to NHRA's first 6-second Pro Stock pass at Englishtown (6.988), allows second-generation driver to win first Pro Stock bonus event; WJ sets national record for speed at Atlanta (197.15); four wins in six final rounds; No. 1 qualifier six times
1995	Wins third NHRA Pro Stock championship; national records for speed and ET at Houston (6.948, 199.15); seven victories in nine final rounds; fourth consecutive Indy win; 14 No. 1–qualifier awards; wins second NHRA Pro Stock bonus event; scores 50th national event win (Seattle)
1996	Wins Pro Stock invitational; five wins in eight finals; eight No. 1–qualifier awards; reaches Pro Stock bonus event final round; KJ uses Warren Johnson horsepower to claim first Indy win
1997	Breaks through 200-mph barrier at Richmond (200.13); first driver in NHRA history to make sub-6.9-second pass at Richmond (6.894); additional national records for ET and/or speed set at Pomona (6.927), Gainesville (199.91), Richmond (6.883, 200.53); four wins in six final rounds; seven starts from the No. 1 spot
1998	Wins fourth NHRA Pro Stock championship; wins career-best 56 elimination rounds; sets top speed at 21 of 22 events; finished in top 5 for 17th consecutive season; logs 100th No. 1–qualifying position (Memphis); Warren Johnson horsepower propels KJ to second career Pro Stock bonus event win
1999	Wins fifth NHRA Pro Stock championship; WJ is first driver in NHRA history to set top speed at every event; wins 75th national event (Atlanta); national record for KJ with WJ power at Richmond (6.840); WJ reaches final round of Pro Stock bonus race

40-Year Snapshot	
Year	**Details**
1970	Homebuilt Pro Stock Camaro campaigned at UDRA events in Midwest
1971	First NHRA Pro Stock race, U.S. Nationals in Indianapolis
1973	Big-block Vega is raced by WJ in AHRA Pro Stock and NHRA B/Altered
1976	Runner-up in NHRA championship; three final-round appearances
1978	First NHRA No. 1 qualifier
1979	First IHRA Pro Stock championship
1980	Second IHRA Pro Stock championship
1981	Johnson family leaves Minnesota for Georgia; WJ wins three IHRA races; makes AHRA's first 7-second Pro Stock run (7.93, St. Louis)
1982	First NHRA Pro Stock victory; first 180-mph Pro Stock run
1983	GM Drag Race Competition Engine (DRCE) introduced in Hurst/Oldsmobile
1984	First U.S. Nationals victory; runner-up in NHRA championship
1985	Five wins in new Calais
1986	First 190-mph Pro Stock run
1987	Winston All-Stars victory
1988	Runner-up in NHRA championship
1989	Cutlass Supreme aero package developed by WJ
1990	Ten top speeds in 19 races
1991	Five victories and runner-up finish in NHRA championship
1992	First NHRA championship; eight wins
1993	WJ and KJ finish 1-2 in standings, win 15 of 18 events; 9 wins in 12 finals for WJ
1995	Third NHRA championship; seven victories
1996	Five victories; No. 2 in championship in new Firebird
1997	First 200-mph run (200.13 mph, Richmond, Virginia)
1998	Fourth NHRA championship; 9 wins in 12 final rounds
1999	Fifth NHRA championship; top speed at every event; seven wins; 15 No. 1 qualifiers
2001	Sixth NHRA championship
2003	22nd consecutive top 10 finish; 22nd consecutive season with a win; perfect 4-0 in finals
2004	WJ introduced GM DRCE-3 engine; 23rd straight season with a final round
2005	School's Out tour; six No. 1 qualifiers; three victories; surpassed 800 career round wins

40-Year Snapshot	
Year	**Details**
2006	500th career NHRA race; win in Phoenix
2007	Inducted into International Motorsports Hall of Fame at Talladega
2008	Top speed at 14 events
2009	Career-best ET and speed (6.561, 211.26 mph)
2010	Earned 97th Pro Stock win
2011	Inducted into the NHRA Division 2 Hall of Fame
2012	Inducted into the Georgia Racing Hall of Fame
2013	Inducted into Bristol Dragway's Legends of Thunder Valley
2014	Inducted into Don Garlits International Drag Racing Hall of Fame
2015	Inducted into Motorsports Hall of Fame of America
2016	Inducted into Mesabi East Athletic Hall of Fame in Aurora, Minnesota

WJ's NHRA Career: By the Numbers

- 649 career NHRA Pro Stock races
- 97 national event wins
- 151 final rounds
- 138 No. 1–qualifier awards
- 874 elimination-round wins
- 220 top-speed-of-the-event records

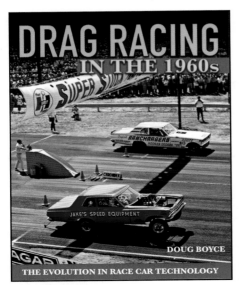

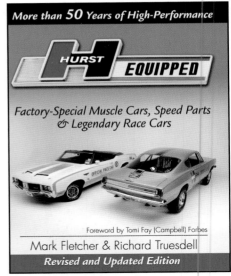
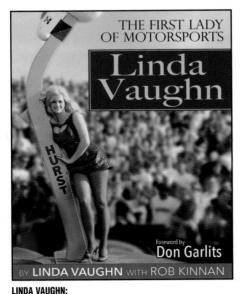